"Reading this book, I am struck by the fact that the Church itself has shown a new face to the wider world in the person of this Jesuit pope with a Franciscan name, a leader with a spirituality and pastoral theology forged on many of the ministerial frontiers named in the book itself. Religious life has always served a prophetic function in the Church, whether it has been lived out by women or men. The chapters of this book accentuate this prophetic dimension of Christian priesthood, not only as it relates to the priestly identity of individual members of religious orders but as it informs ministerial collaboration among all ordained and lay leaders in the Church."

    —Christopher Hadley, SJ
    Jesuit School of Theology

"When Hollywood occasionally portrays a Catholic priest on film, the specter of Bing Crosby in 'Going My Way' still lingers. Usually that priest is a parish priest, living a solitary life in the rectory and worrying about the upkeep of the school. In fact, as recent history has shown, many diocesan bishops and even higher church officials have the same image in mind. This superb volume of essays reminds us that, although there is one priesthood, it has two very different expressions. Drawing on experience, sociological data, and sound theology and history, these well-informed essays illustrate the distinctive—and necessary—contribution that priesthood in a religious context offers to the life of the church. Religious priests represent a diverse, prophetic, and collegial experience of priesthood, rooted in the charisms of their respective communities and flourishing in a wide array of ministries."

    —Donald Senior, CP
    President Emeritus and Chancellor
    Catholic Theological Union, Chicago

"This book calls religious priests to embrace the tension between profession and ordination in order to re-embrace the mercy at the heart of many of the founders of religious orders. This book highlights the mobility that allows religious to transcend both diocesan boundaries and cultural boundaries in order to forge new ways of discipleship for encountering a world of change revved up by the almost daily innovations of technology. This book is indispensable for anyone interested in the religious priesthood in the twenty-first century, and I cannot recommend it highly enough!"

— Garrett Galvin, OFM
Franciscan School of Theology

"This book represents a deep and remarkably insightful integration of the past and the future in that it offers a vision of a prophetic and servant model of priesthood rooted in intercultural and international modes of religious life. I believe that this project not only points the way to the future of the religious life and ordained ministry, but also for the universal church and its own mission to 'read the signs of the times' and evolve as a truly inculturated prophetic and priestly community in the contemporary world."

— John J. Markey, OP
Oblate School of Theology

Priesthood in Religious Life

Searching for New Ways Forward

Edited by Stephen Bevans, SVD,
and Robin Ryan, CP

LITURGICAL PRESS
Collegeville, Minnesota

www.litpress.org

1   2   3   4   5   6   7   8   9

Library of Congress Cataloging-in-Publication Data

Names: Bevans, Stephen B., 1944– editor. | Ryan, Robin, editor.
Title: Priesthood in religious life : searching for new ways forward / edited by Stephen Bevans, SVD and Robin Ryan, CP.
Description: Collegeville, Minnesota : Liturgical Press, [2018] | Includes bibliographical references.
Identifiers: LCCN 2018016786 (print) | LCCN 2018036738 (ebook) | ISBN 9780814684788 (ebook) | ISBN 9780814684542
Subjects: LCSH: Priesthood—Catholic Church. | Priests—Religious life.
Classification: LCC BX1912 (ebook) | LCC BX1912 .P7524 2018 (print) | DDC 262/.142—dc23
LC record available at https://lccn.loc.gov/2018016786

Contents

Preface

It is with great delight that I welcome you to *Priesthood in Religious Life: Searching for New Ways Forward*. This book is the fruit of a marvelous April 2017 conference by the same name, sponsored by the Center for the Study of Consecrated Life (CSCL) at Catholic Theological Union, Chicago. This is the first book to come from the proceedings of a CSCL conference, and our hope is that it is the first of many such printed contributions to consecrated life today.

The mission of the CSCL is to serve as a theological, academic, and pastoral resource on contemporary topics and issues related to consecrated life. This book serves to contribute to and foster further conversations about the role of priesthood in religious life. Such discussions deepen one's own vocation to religious life, assist others to understand this particular call, and may create opportunities for bishops and religious priests to dialogue further about such a call. First and foremost, though, the desire is to deepen understandings of and the living of the service of priesthood in religious life. As such, the book engages many contexts, and it covers various topics related to culture, charism, spirituality, and ministry. The diversity of authors in this volume brings forth necessary voices and widens and deepens our perspectives on religious life and priesthood today.

I am grateful to Stephen Bevans, SVD, who led this project, organizing a wonderful conference attended by over two hundred people from all over the United States, and who was an editor of this volume. I am also very grateful to Robin Ryan, CP, the other editor of this volume. Immense gratitude also goes to the essay contributors. Each and every one has helped us in the search for new ways forward in the call of religious priesthood in our church and world. This engagement of their vocations calls each of us more deeply in our own vocations.

Enjoy—and engage!

Maria Cimperman, RSCJ
Director
Center for the Study of Consecrated Life
Catholic Theological Union, Chicago

Introduction

A Priesthood Shaped by Religious Life

Stephen Bevans, SVD, and Robin Ryan, CP

On April 6–7, 2017, the Center for the Study of Consecrated Life (CSCL) at Catholic Theological Union (CTU) held a major conference entitled "Priesthood in Religious Life: Searching for New Ways Forward." The response to invitations to attend the conference from priesthood candidates at CTU, from members of many religious congregations that make up the "Union" for which CTU is named, and from religious priesthood candidates and religious priests and brothers from other parts of North America was fairly overwhelming. Some 225 persons gathered at the opening session of the conference, signaling that the CSCL had hit upon a topic of immense interest to religious today, and in particular to those congregations whose membership includes persons who are ordained.

Because of this interest, we are so pleased to offer the reflections and findings of our conference to a wider public. We hope that the readers of this volume will find its contents helpful in their own search for ways forward in better understanding and living out the charism of ordained ministry within religious life. We also hope that they will join other religious—in community discussion groups, in further conferences, in blogs, in more scholarly reflection and research—in the search for a deeper understanding of this distinct form of Christian service.

Of course, the search that our conference and this volume have undertaken is not at all new. It is a continuation of a search for a more distinct understanding and practice of ordained ministry that has emerged over the last several decades among members of religious congregations. While the theology of priesthood articulated at the Second Vatican Council provided a much-needed reform of priestly ministry and life, ordained ministers in religious life have found its perspectives more and more inadequate. The move from the Tridentine cultic understanding of the priest as the one who offered sacrifice and forgave sins[1] to a more pastoral model of the priest as participating in Christ's headship of the church as priest, prophet, and servant leader[2] was certainly crucial to a renewed understanding of ordained ministry. However, as church historian John O'Malley points out in a landmark article on priesthood in religious life, Vatican II's dominant image of the priest is that of the diocesan priest, in communion with the bishop of his particular church and ministering in or pastoring a parish.[3] Even though the council's document on priesthood does mention priests who are religious, it focuses on what diocesan and religious priests have in common rather than on how, in the exercise of the priesthood, they are distinct from one another (see PO 1).

In his opening keynote address at our conference, Newark's Cardinal Joseph Tobin expressed in a particularly striking way the malaise that religious priests have come to feel regarding their distinctness as *religious* priests. Tobin is a member of the Congregation of the Holy Redeemer, or Redemptorists, and served from 1997 until 2009 as its superior general. He noted that on his visits to Redemptorist communities around the world, he would often encounter a diocesan bishop who would praise the Redemptorists working in his diocese. They were as much a part of the diocese, the bishop would say, as any of his diocesan priests. The bishop would observe that he could hardly tell the difference. Tobin wryly remarked that while the bishop certainly meant this as a compliment to him and the Redemptorist priests working in the diocese, it was a remark that disturbed him, as superior general of a religious congregation, quite profoundly.

1. Denzinger/Schönmetzer, *Enchiridion Symbolorum: Definitionum et Declarationum de Rebus Fidei et Morum*, 34th ed. (Barcinone: Herder, 1967), #1764.

2. Vatican Council II, Decree on the Ministry and Life of Priests, *Presbyterorum Ordinis* (PO), 1–2.

3. John W. O'Malley, "Priesthood, Ministry, and Religious Life: Some Historical and Historiographical Considerations," *Theological Studies* 49, no. 2 (1988): 223–24.

Was there no distinctive way in which Redemptorists lived out their ministry as priests and so were able to bring a distinctive contribution to their missionary service?

Here in the United States (the context in which our conference took place[4]), the inadequacy of—or even the disregard for—such distinction has been further aggravated by developments in the *Program of Priestly Formation* (*PPF*). There has been a move in the document from greater acknowledgment of the "pluriform" nature of religious and diocesan priesthood in its first two editions to a much lesser acknowledgment of difference in the last three. Franciscan sister Katarina Schuth traces this development in her chapter in this volume. As a result of this development, as Franciscan Leslie Hoppe notes in his contribution, bishops who participated in the papal visitations of seminaries in 1981 and 2002[5] simply did not understand the style of formation for priesthood in schools of theology where religious were being trained. Hoppe's chapter explains how the Conference of Major Superiors of Men (CMSM) attempted to produce their own *PPF*, an attempt that resulted in the important document *The Gift of Religious Priesthood: Formation for Presbyteral Ministry in Institutes of Religious Life.*[6]

In the years since Vatican II there have been a good number of efforts to explore the distinct nature of priesthood in religious life. In the United States, CMSM began to receive requests to study the distinctiveness of priesthood in religious life in the early 1980s, especially in light of growing requests by bishops for religious to take over diocesan parishes because of the shortage of diocesan priests.[7] During the 1980s several landmark articles appeared, most notably

---

4. It should be noted, however, that Timothy Scott, CSB, offered a workshop on religious priesthood in the Canadian context. His workshop paper appears as chapter 13 of this volume.

5. Donald W. Wuerl, "Seminary Visitation," *America*, September 30, 2002, https://www.americamagazine.org/issue/403/article/seminary-visitation.

6. As Hoppe references the document at the end of his article, it can be found at http://cmsm.org/wp-content/uploads/2016/07/FormationReligious PriestsOct2011.pdf.

7. Paul K. Hennessy, "Introduction: The Parochialization of the Church and Consecrated Life," in *A Concert of Charisms: Ordained Ministry in Religious Life*, ed. Paul K. Hennessy (New York/Mahwah, NJ: Paulist Press, 1997), 4.

those of Jesuits Brian E. Daley and John W. O'Malley, both published in the prestigious journal *Theological Studies*.[8] In 1990 the CMSM began a process, first at the regional level and then at the national, to reflect on the question of priesthood in religious life. There were a number of consultations held in various venues around the United States, and the results of the process were published in 1997 in the book *A Concert of Charisms: Ordained Ministry in Religious Life*.[9] To our knowledge, this important volume—with significant contributions by Jesuit John W. O'Malley, Benedictine Kevin Seasoltz, Dominican Paul Philibert, Oblate David Power, and Mercy sister Doris Gottemoeller, among others—is the last major contribution to the discussion about priesthood in religious life published in the United States. Major contributions to the discussion were published in both Italian and Spanish in 2010,[10] but this present volume is the first book-length study of the question in English in the last twenty years.

The basic conviction that the studies and reflections of the past decades have brought to the discussion is that priesthood in religious life is a ministry *shaped* by religious life. Whereas, as the late Dominican Paul Philibert never tired of pointing out, diocesan priests take priesthood as their primary identity, religious priests find their identity first and foremost in the community life, the vows, and the particular charism or cluster of charisms of their particular religious congregation.[11] Religious priesthood needs to be rooted in the rich theology of brotherhood that Capuchin John Pavlik explores in his

8. Brian E. Daley, "The Ministry of Disciples: Historical Reflections on the Role of Religious Priests," *Theological Studies* 48 (1987): 605–29; O'Malley, "Priesthood, Ministry, and Religious Life," 223–57.

9. Hennessy, "Introduction," 5.

10. Rossano Zas Friz de Col, *Il presbitero religioso nella chiesa* (Bologna: Edizioni Dehoniane, 2010); A. Bocos Merino, S. del Cura Elena, J. C. R. García Paredes, Mos. G. A. Gardin, J. Rodríguez Carballo, *Ministros ordenados religiosos: Situación—Carisma—Servicio* (Madrid: Publicaciones Claretianas, 2010). The Spanish volume includes a nine-page bibliography.

11. Paul Philibert in "Religious Priesthood: Issues and Concerns for Renewal," in *The Charism of Priesthood: Diocesan and Religious Priests Together in Ministry* (Chicago: National Federation of Priests' Councils, 1996), 11; see also Paul Philibert, "Priesthood within the Context of Religious Life," in *Being a Priest Today*, ed. Donald Goergen (Collegeville, MN: Liturgical Press, A Michael Glazier Book, 1992), 73–96.

chapter in these pages. Ed Hahnenberg's keynote address at the conference warned the assembly not to get caught in a "blueprint ecclesiology" that would restrict the imagination in terms of the possibilities of a priesthood shaped by religious life. Religious should actually ask themselves what their experiences of priesthood are as they live it out as members of their communities. Religious life might offer an understanding of priesthood that "doesn't fit" within a neatly articulated theology of the ordained ministry, and yet would contribute mightily to the overall mission of the church. Emphasizing the communal, community nature of religious life, SCJ canonist David Szatkowski's chapter suggests that canon 517 §1's option of "*in solidum*" "when circumstances require" might provide a way of organizing a parish that could spotlight the nonhierarchical, fraternal nature of a male religious community. Spiritan anthropologist Anthony Gittins's reflections on cross-culturality suggest that priesthood might be shaped by a strong commitment to cross-cultural life in community and in the choices and style of ministry in which a religious priest will engage. While Robin Ryan admits that Pope Francis does not often specifically speak of *religious* priesthood in his communications, the pope's own perspective as a Jesuit, we believe, surely shapes his insistence on a priesthood that refuses to be caught up in careerism and clericalism and spends itself in close collaboration with ordinary Christian people.

An aspect of religious priesthood that has been rather underexplored in the literature is the contribution that culture might make to the shape of priesthood in religious life today. Given the commitment to intercultural living and mission that is central to both Catholic Theological Union and its Center for the Study of Consecrated Life, it was natural that several workshop presentations should search for new ways forward in this important direction. Redemptorist Maurice Nutt offers here a touching testimony to his love of his religious community, despite its unintentional disregard of his African American culture, and how it has nevertheless shaped his priestly ministry. One suggestion he makes is that, given the large percentage of African Americans who are pastored by Protestant, Evangelical, and Pentecostal ministers, African American religious priests might emphasize the importance of ecumenical activities and involvement. Claretian Eddie De León reflects on his experience as a Puerto Rican/ Latinx religious and calls for an exercise of priesthood that is "prophetic." Such prophetic priesthood would put more emphasis on effective, contextual preaching (an emphasis that appears in Franciscan Daniel Horan's chapter as well), would be a sign of hope for women and men on the margins of society, and would be fearless in confronting injustice, racism, and prejudice. SVD New Testament scholar vănThanh Nguyễn offers the very Asian image of a bamboo plant/tree to describe what religious priesthood might mean in the Asian-American context. Emphasizing in particular the charism of interculturality of his own highly multicultural and international community, Nguyễn highlights the need for Asian-American religious to exercise ordained ministry with gentle strength that comes with flexibility and is rooted, like the complex root system of the bamboo, in communal and cultural identity.

While these cultural perspectives shed light on how priesthood in religious life could be lived out distinctively by African Americans, Latinxs, and Asian-Americans, we believe that they shed light as well on how religious priesthood can be lived out distinctively in general, across the board, by members of all ethnic groups. Strong ecumenical and interfaith commitments, prophetic commitment that goes beyond a more cultic understanding of priesthood, and a commitment to fostering real interculturality in their communities are features of priesthood that might be espoused by religious men who choose to live out their religious life in a life of ordained ministry.

We have already referred to Capuchin John Pavlik's chapter on the theology of religious brotherhood. Consciousness and acceptance of one's brotherhood and the equality that it fosters can root the religious who is a priest within his identity as a brother to every member of his religious community. Another aspect of emphasizing such brotherhood is the perduring lay character of religious priesthood despite its belonging to the clerical state and ecclesiastical hierarchy. With its origins in lay movements of radical Christian life, religious life never loses its lay character,[12] even, we believe, if the

---

12. In an often-quoted line, for example, the fourth-century monk John Cassian repeated what he called "an old maxim of the fathers": that "a monk ought by all means to fly from women and bishops." Quoted in John W. O'Malley, "One Priesthood: Two Traditions," in *A Concert of Charisms*, ed. Hennessy, 9. See John Cassian, *De institutis coenobiorum et de octo principalium vitiorum remediis* XI, 18 (in *Sources chrétiennes*, ed. J.-C. Guy, 108.444).

religious enters ordained ministry. This lay, nonclerical character of priesthood in religious life is particularly apparent in communities in which nonordained members (brothers) and ordained members (deacons, priests) live and work together.

An effect of this lay orientation of religious presbyteral ministry might well be a ministry that pays particular attention to and cultivates lay ministries in the church—both "ordinary" lay ministries like lectoring or bringing communion to the sick and "lay ecclesial" ministries that require more formal training and special commissioning in the church. Parish ministry, hospital ministry, retreat ministry, or social justice ministry that is led by a religious who is a priest holds the "missionary discipleship" of every member in high esteem, gives every member a voice in decision making, and encourages every member to develop and grow. Indeed, ecclesiology has begun to reflect in more recent times the notion of "discipleship" (or "missionary discipleship" as Pope Francis seems to prefer[13]) as a way of speaking that transcends the lay-clerical distinction, rooting Christian ministry and life in the basic dignity and equality bestowed by baptism.[14] Along the same lines of Daniel Horan's argument that religious priests might emphasize particular components of the *tria munera* of Christ's priestly (cultic), prophetic, and governing (servant leadership) office, such focus on baptismal discipleship might point to religious priests' particular focus (without neglecting the other two *munera*) on a style of leadership that calls forth the gifts of all the people among whom they work.

Building on Horan's and Eddie De León's insights about a particular focus by religious priests on the *prophetic* aspect of Christ's threefold office, we might speak as well of a prophetic priesthood in religious life that offers critique to the more institutional structures

13. Francis, *Evangelii Gaudium* (EG) (The Joy of the Gospel), apostolic exhortation (Vatican City, Libreria Editrice Vatican, 2013), 24, https://w2.vatican.va/content/francesco/en/apost_exhortations/documents/papa-francesco_esortazione-ap_20131124_evangelii-gaudium.html.

14. EG 104. See Vatican Council II, Dogmatic Constitution on the Church, *Lumen Gentium* (LG) 32; Richard R. Gaillardetz, *Ecclesiology for a Global Church: A People Called and Sent* (Maryknoll, NY: Orbis Books, 2008), 173–207; and Kathleen Cahalan, *Introduction to the Practice of Ministry* (Collegeville, MN: Liturgical Press, 2010).

and practices that diocesan priesthood necessarily supports. As Yves Congar argued decades ago, the church needs the charismatic aspect of religious life to constantly challenge its institutional life.[15] While always remaining loyal to the episcopal leadership of the church, priests who are religious might call into question structures and practices that seem to benefit the institution or the clerical state more than the mission of the church and its service of the gospel. That Pope Francis has spoken out so strongly for a more missionary church and against clerical privilege may well be rooted, as we have noted, in his own identity as a religious. Religious who are pastors might push certain legitimate practices to their limits—for example, lay preaching under certain circumstances or sensitivity to culture and context in liturgical celebrations. They might embrace other legitimate practices that are not often taken advantage of, such as encouraging a more active (although still consultative) parish pastoral council, employing more qualified lay ministers, or developing stronger ties with other Christians and people of other faiths by means of common worship services when possible, common worship space, and common acts for social and ecological justice.

In his 1996 apostolic exhortation *Vita Consecrata*, Pope St. John Paul II observed that "in the [religious] priest, the vocation to the priesthood and the vocation to the consecrated life converge in a profound and dynamic unity."[16] By this statement, we believe, the pope did not mean that priesthood in religious life is a "better" state of life than religious life as such. Nor did he mean that religious priesthood is somehow a better way to live out the vocation of ordained ministry than "mere" diocesan priesthood. What we think John Paul II was indicating is that priesthood in religious life does have a *distinct* identity. It is not necessarily a *unique* identity, in that diocesan priests can also be rooted in a community of presbyters, or can be particularly inclusive of laypeople in their ministry, or can be prophetic figures in the church, or can be experts in calling forth intercultural parish communities. What makes religious priests dis-

15. Yves Congar, *True and False Reform in the Church*, trans. Paul Philibert (Collegeville, MN: Liturgical Press, 2011), 249–54. Originally published in 1950.

16. John Paul II, *Vita Consecrata*, post-synodal apostolic exhortation (Vatican City, Libreria Editrice Vatican, 1996), 30.

tinct is the call to shape their priesthood according to the values and traditions of religious life, to be profoundly shaped by what Sandra Schneiders calls the "life form" of religious life, which is in turn shaped by community, vows, charism, and—for many—active ministry.[17] As a former SVD provincial was wont to say, SVD identity is not about being totally *unique or different from* other congregations. Rather, it is about being *faithful* to the particular charisms with which the Society of the Divine Word has been gifted. In the same way, we think, a distinct religious priesthood can emerge as ordained religious are faithful to their community-centered, vowed, and charism-inspired identities in their particular congregations. Their priesthood, in other words, would emerge as a priesthood *shaped* by religious life.

Contemporary ecclesiology's reflections on discipleship can shed light on how this distinction is just that—a distinction, not a designation of a better or fuller or more radical way of life as such. We are all disciples, and as disciples we are all radically equal. But the discipleship we share in common is constituted by a variety of gifts, all of which are necessary for the whole and yet all of which differ—in intensity, in scope, in responsibility. The CMSM document on which Leslie Hoppe reflects gets it right: priesthood in religious life is indeed a gift given to some, but not to set them apart from or above the rest. Rather, religious priesthood is a gift for the building up of the entire church.

As we bring this book to publication, we want to acknowledge the leadership of Mark Francis, CSV, president of CTU, and of Barbara Reid, OP, vice president and academic dean. We are grateful as well for the leadership and support of Maria Cimperman, RSCJ, director of the CSCL and author of the preface to this volume. We are thankful to so many on the CTU staff who helped in the planning of the April 2017 conference from which this book has been developed,

---

17. The definition comes from a handout given by Sandra Schneiders at a workshop on religious life. See Marilyn King, RSM, "Are We Fascinating? Religious Life as a Prophetic Life Form," http://www.mercyworld.org/_uploads/_cknw/files/2015/2-King_Are%20We%20fascinating.pdf; Sandra Schneiders, "Religious Life as Prophetic Life Form," https://www.ursulines-ur.org/phocadownload/userupload/Resources/propheticlifeform.pdf.

and to the keynote speakers and workshop leaders who made the conference such a memorable event. Our thanks go as well to Br. Michael O'Neill McGrath, ST, for permission to use his painting "High Priest" on our book's cover. McGrath's painting graced announcements of our conference, appeared on the cover of the program, and was projected on screens in the conference hall. The painting's depiction of Christ exercising his priesthood by washing the feet of humanity in all its variety seems to us a particularly powerful image of a priesthood that is shaped by a vowed life lived in community for prophetic witness in our world. Finally, we are deeply grateful to Hans Christoffersen of Liturgical Press, who has helped bring this book to publication.

We hope, as we offer the proceedings of a wonderful conference to a general audience, that this book will indeed help the women and men of the entire church in their search for ways forward in understanding and living out the great gift that is priesthood in religious life.

Chapter 1

A Bishop's Perspective on Priesthood in Religious Life

Cardinal Joseph Tobin, CSsR

Introduction

I am grateful for an opportunity to reflect on the service of ordained members of religious institutes in the light of the global theme of this conference: "Priesthood in Religious Life: Searching for New Ways Forward." There is no doubt that this theme offers a number of interesting questions. Allow me to suggest a few.

First, what is the ecclesial identity and mission of religious priesthood? More precisely, how is the vocation of religious priesthood distinct from, and how does it overlap with, the vocations of nonordained religious and nonreligious priests? Is religious priesthood merely a hybrid of religious life and priesthood, or does it have its own integrity as a differentiated charismatic mission?

Secondly, does the vocation to religious priesthood compromise either the vocation to religious life or the vocation to priesthood? If not, why not?[1]

---

1. Professor Daniel Christian Raab, OSB, uses these two questions to introduce his doctoral thesis "Compromise or Charism?: The Identity and Mission of Religious Priesthood in Light of Hans Urs von Balthasar's Theology" (Washington, DC: Catholic University of America, 2015), 1. I am grateful to Professor Raab for making a copy available to me.

1

While it is possible to identify theologies and spiritualities that are more amenable to the notion of ordained religious, in my personal experience, as well as that of most religious priests I know, there is an undeniable tension between one's profession and one's ordination. I do not believe the object of this symposium should be the elimination of such tension. I hope that our conversation over the next two days will illuminate the reality of the unique path of religious priesthood and thereby assure those called to walk it that the tension in our lives will remain creative.

Someone observed, "You can tell the preacher's sins by what he preaches about." I hope you will allow me to forgo a treatment of the fundamental questions regarding the theological basis for religious priesthood in favor of a modest discussion of a relationship that has interested me for many years. A memory from my service as consultor general and superior general of my religious institute, the Redemptorist Missionaries, may help you understand the topic I intend to present.

During the eighteen years I served in the general council, I was privileged to visit communities in seventy of the seventy-eight countries where my confreres are missioned. I thus had many occasions to listen to a diocesan bishop describe the situation of the Redemptorists in a particular church. Often the ordinary would assure me with evident satisfaction that there were no problems with the confreres. "In fact," he might add, "unless I really think about it, I cannot distinguish your confreres from the diocesan clergy." For some diocesan bishops, that sort of assimilation appears to be good news; a superior general would arrive at a different conclusion. So would Pope St. John Paul II, who expected that "the charisms of the consecrated life can greatly contribute to the building up of charity in the particular Churches."[2]

So what I would like to consider with you is the relationship of the charism of religious priests and the particular church by focusing on two questions. First, in what sense are religious priests members of a diocesan presbyterate? I propose that we begin with number 8

2. John Paul II, *Vita Consecrata*, post-synodal apostolic exhortation (Vatican City: Libreria Editrice Vaticana, 1996), 48.

of Vatican II's Decree on the Life and Ministry of Priests, *Presbyterorum Ordinis* (PO),[3] which provides a fundamental orientation. I will trace the postconciliar development of this doctrine in other documents of the magisterium, giving particular attention to the instruction *Mutuae Relationes* (MR).[4]

Secondly, what does the pastor of a particular church need to keep in mind as he coordinates the charismatic gifts that should enrich the people of God? Here I am particularly interested in a proper understanding of canon 586 §1, which attributes to institutes of consecrated life a "just autonomy." While the canon situates this autonomy in the area of internal governance, I will argue that it should condition the way that the ministry of ordained priests is incorporated into the pastoral plan of the particular church.

Let us begin, then, with a consideration of the first question: what is the relationship between religious priests and the diocesan presbyterate?

Religious Priests and the Diocesan Presbyterate: A Rereading of *Presbyterorum Ordinis* 8

Elements

The conciliar Decree on the Life and Ministry of Priests *Presbyterorum Ordinis* begins with a consideration of the role of priests in the mission of the church. After beginning with some thoughts regarding the nature of priesthood and situating the order of priests within the broader context of the people of God, the decree tries to identify the functions of this vocation. The relationship among the ordained is acknowledged to be critical. Number 8 insists that "it is of great importance that all priests, whether diocesan or [religious], should help each other, so that they may be fellow-workers in the service of

---

3. Second Vatican Council, Decree on the Ministry and Life of Priests *Presbyterorum Ordinis* (December 7, 1965).

4. Sacred Congregation for Religious and for Secular Institutes and Sacred Congregation for Bishops, *Directives for the Mutual Relations between Bishops and Religious in the Church* (Roma: 14 May 1978).

truth. Each is joined to the rest of the members of this priestly body by special ties of apostolic charity, of ministry and of fellowship."[5]

The decree attributes a fundamental unity to the ordained priesthood and hopes that priests, whether diocesan or religious, will support each other towards the goal of being always "fellow-workers in the truth." The formula "whether . . . or" clearly recognizes as legitimate two ways of living priesthood: as diocesan priests or ordained religious. From a theological point of view, there can be no doubt about the truth of the affirmation; hence, there would not be the slightest difficulty in applying the doctrine of the decree to all presbyters.

On the other hand, in the practical order, this unity is also a goal to be achieved within the pastoral context of a particular church. Here we can see a particular challenge for religious priests—that is, how they will live the conjunction *and*: religious *and* priest. In other words, how do religious successfully articulate both their participation in the sacrament of Holy Orders and the special consecration of religious life?

Beyond recognizing the fundamental unity of all priests in one presbyterium, it seems useful to highlight two other elements in number 8 of *Presbyterorum Ordinis*. First, there is an exhortation that is original, even generative: "that all priests . . . help one another always to be fellow workers in the truth" (i.e., "cooperatores veritatis"). Beyond hearing in this phrase a reference to the third Johannine epistle,[6] today one cannot help but think of Pope Benedict XVI, who chose the phrase as his episcopal motto. The phrase also offers a paradigm for relationships among ministers at all levels of the church communion.

Secondly, if it is true that the problem of the unity of the presbyterium is to be situated primarily in the practical rather than doctrinal sphere, the three "special bonds" that should exist among

5. "Quapropter magni momenti est ut omnes Presbyteri, sive diocesani sive religiosi, sese invicem adiuvent, ut semper sint cooperatores veritatis. Cum ceteris ergo membris huius Presbyterii, unusquisque specialibus apostolicae caritatis, ministerii et fraternitatis nexibus coniungitur" (PO 8).

6. "Therefore, we ought to support such persons, so that we may be co-workers in the truth" (3 John 1:8).

ordained priests, "apostolic charity, ministry and fellowship," will help all priests make visible and credible such accord.

The Road after the Council

Instruction Mutuae Relationes

Commenting on the origins of the instruction *Mutuae Relationes*, Cardinal Eduardo Pironio, at the time the prefect of the Sacred Congregation for Religious and Secular Institutes, highlighted the spirit that guided the preparation of the document. It was born "from a deeper appreciation of the mystery of the Church as the 'new People of God' as well as the urgency for more effective coordination of the different charisms and pastoral ministries."[7] The dynamism that permeates the whole document is a strong impulse of the Holy Spirit within the church and "the principle of unity in communion."[8]

The instruction *Mutuae Relationes* does not hesitate to insert religious priests into the one presbyterium, even if there is no reference to the above-cited number of *Presbyterorum Ordinis*. Instead, the fundamental unity of the presbyterium is posited by appeal to the Dogmatic Constitution on the Church, *Lumen Gentium* (LG), and to the Decree on the Pastoral Office of Bishops, *Christus Dominus* (CD): "Religious priests, by virtue of the very unity of the priesthood (cf. LG 28; CD 28; 11) and inasmuch as they share in the care of souls, 'may be said, in a certain sense, to belong to the diocesan clergy' (CD 34); therefore, in the field of activity, they can and should serve to unite and coordinate religious men and women with the local clergy and bishop" (MR 36).

One can see how the fact of the unity of the presbyterium and its coresponsibility for the *cura animarum* create bonds that unite religious priests with the diocesan presbyterium. A further task is assigned to religious priests: that of serving as a sort of bridge to other members of the consecrated life in the local church with an aim to strengthening and expanding the participation of all in the

---

7. Ángel Aparicio, ed., *La vida consagrada: Documentos conciliares y postconciliares*, 4th ed. (Madrid: Publicaciones Claretianas, 2009), 170 [my translation].
8. Ibid., 171.

mission of the diocese. Finally, the instruction asserts that the attitude of the members of the presbyterium as well as the structures of the local church should witness to a tangible appreciation for members of the consecrated life.[9]

Apostolic Exhortation Vita Consecrata

Vita Consecrata (VC), the apostolic exhortation that brought to completion the work of the Synod of Bishops on Consecrated Life,[10] in number 48 gave particular attention to the relationship between religious and the local church. Although Pope John Paul II is speaking about consecrated people in general and does not refer specifically to the relationship of religious priests to the diocesan presbyterium, it is not hard to apply the broad vision of the Holy Father to that particular bond. Let us examine briefly the content of number 48 of *Vita Consecrata.*

Consecrated persons play a "significant role" within the local churches, to which the conciliar doctrine regarding the church as mystery and communion attributes the full presence of a portion of the people of God. In the years following Vatican II, the importance of this role has been confirmed by various documents of the magisterium. These texts illustrate clearly "the fundamental importance of cooperation between consecrated persons and Bishops for the organic development of diocesan pastoral life" (VC 48). The charisms of the consecrated life can greatly contribute to "the building up of charity in the particular Churches."

The church recognizes the "rightful autonomy" that is enjoyed by institutes of consecrated life; for their part, bishops "should preserve and safeguard this autonomy." Bishops are asked also "to welcome and esteem the charisms of the consecrated life, and to give them a

---

9. "In order that the diocesan presbyterium express due unity and that the various ministries be better fostered, the bishop should, with all solicitude, exhort the diocesan priests to recognize gratefully the fruitful contribution made by religious to their Church and to approve willingly their nomination to positions of greater responsibility, which are consonant with their vocation and competency" (MR 55).

10. IX Ordinary General Assembly of the Synod of Bishops met October 2–29, 1994, and studied the theme *The Consecrated Life and Its Role in the Church and in the World.*

place in the pastoral plans of the Diocese. They should have a particular concern for Institutes of diocesan right, which are entrusted to the special care of the local Bishop" (VC 48)[11]

Pastores Dabo Vobis *and* Pastores Gregis

The apostolic exhortations that followed the Synods on the Formation of Priests (1–28 October 1990) and the Office of Bishop (30 September–27 October 2001) do not contribute directly to our discussion. Even though John Paul II introduces *Pastores Dabo Vobis* (PDV)[12] by expressing his desire through this exhortation "to meet with each and every priest, whether diocesan or religious" (4), he does not develop further the relationship between religious and diocesan priests.

Pastores Gregis (PG),[13] the exhortation that concluded the Synod on the Office of Bishop, invites the diocesan ordinary to display pastoral care for consecrated life with an aim of promoting greater communion within the particular church (21, 22, 48), and it refers to a concrete problem between bishops and missionary institutes (65). There is no specific treatment of religious priests as members of the diocesan presbyterium.

In summary, while the magisterium has made efforts to develop the conciliar vision of the church as a mystery of communion, it appears that the relationship between religious priests and the presbyterium of the diocese has not had a prominent place in this theological reflection. The affirmations of the council (cf. PO 8; LG 28; CD 28, 11) on the relationship among priests, whether religious or diocesan, in the presbyterium are not echoed in postconciliar documents, save the important exception of the instruction *Mutuae Relationes*.[14]

Now I want to address the manner in which religious, particularly those who are ordained, are inserted into a particular church.

11. See also numbers 49–50 for a broader exposition on the role of religious in the communion of the particular church.

12. John Paul II, *Pastores Dabo Vobis*, post-synodal apostolic exhortation (Vatican City: Libreria Editrice Vaticana, 1992).

13. John Paul II, *Pastores Gregis*, post-synodal apostolic exhortation (Vatican City: Libreria Editrice Vaticana, 2003).

14. Cf. n. 8 above.

Consecrated Life and the Particular Church

In the wake of Vatican II, both the theology of the particular church and that of consecrated life have developed significantly. However, such development has not been accompanied by a successful integration of the two.

Here I would simply note two matters that call for further reflection, even experimentation:

- On the one hand, consecrated life needs to be inserted adequately within the particular church, since it is within a particular church that it lives and that the universal church is made present ("in quibus et ex quibus [Ecclesiis particularibus] unica et una Ecclesia catholica exsistit" [LG 23]).

- On the other hand, it should not be forgotten that consecrated life is called to witness to the universal church within the reality of a particular church. The apostolic exhortation *Vita Consecrata* clearly affirms this mission.[15]

In effect, different particular churches, especially in Asia and Africa, have experienced directly the contribution of religious men and women who came from other dioceses and were present at the birth and growing years of these young churches. In addition, religious frequently bring to their diocese of origin requests for help for these young churches and thus can favor a real "exchange of gifts."

Hence, the bishop should avoid—if I might be permitted a neologism—an excessive "diocesization" of consecrated life, that is, acting as if a religious institute, which is by nature international, instead is only a function of a particular church. It is interesting to note that Proposition 29 of the Synod of Bishops on Consecrated Life recom-

---

15. "All this brings out the character of universality and communion proper to Institutes of Consecrated Life and to Societies of Apostolic Life. Because of their supra-diocesan character, grounded in their special relation to the Petrine ministry, they are also at the service of cooperation between the particular churches, since they can effectively promote an 'exchange of gifts' among them, and thus contribute to an inculturation of the Gospel, which purifies, strengthens and ennobles the treasures found in the cultures of all peoples" (VC 47).

mended that religious give greater attention to the particular church and that bishops value and welcome the charism of consecrated life, making room for religious within the pastoral plan of the diocese.

What does this mean, in practical terms, for the relationship of religious priests and a particular church?

- First, there is a need for mutual respect and effective communication between the diocesan bishop and the major superiors of religious priests who serve in the diocese. A bishop should treat serious matters with the major superior instead of limiting his communication to the local superior, pastor, school director, etc.

- The diocesan bishop will want to identify with major superiors different occasions for regular communication as well as promote extraordinary celebrations, such as the annual commemoration of consecrated life (February 2). Reciprocal visits have also proven to be helpful in fostering communion between the diocesan bishop and religious.

- The bishop ought to appreciate persons and structures, such as the diocesan vicar or delegate for consecrated life, that will enhance his pastoral care for religious.

- The bishop may wish to include religious in some of the diocesan offices or consultative bodies such as presbyteral or pastoral councils.

The Autonomy of Religious

As is the case with nonordained forms of consecrated life, a particular church, particularly its pastor, needs to acknowledge the autonomy of religious life. Canon 586 §1 of the Code of Canon Law recognizes a "just autonomy of life, especially of governance"[16] for institutes of consecrated life; canon 732 calls for a similar recognition in the case

---

16. "Singulis institutis iusta autonomia vitae, praesertim regiminis, agnoscitur, qua gaudeant in Ecclesia propria disciplina atque integrum servare valeant suum patrimonium, de quo in can. 578."

of societies of apostolic life.[17] This autonomy is the means by which a single institute of consecrated life or society of apostolic life can enjoy in the church its own internal discipline and preserve intact its proper charism and identity.[18]

With regard to their proper bishop, a "just autonomy" is attributed also to institutes and societies of diocesan right by canon 594, which judges as illegitimate any interference by the bishop in the internal life of the institute. The local ordinary is charged with safeguarding and protecting the just autonomy of institutes of either pontifical or diocesan right that are present in the diocese.[19]

Hence, the bishop is never considered the superior of an institute. Even in the case of institutes of diocesan right, the Code never applies to the bishop any title that is proper to a religious superior, such as "moderator." The preferred phrase is typically something like "[The institute] remains under the 'special care' of the diocesan bishop."[20]

The just autonomy of institutes of consecrated life and societies of apostolic life should not be understood simply as respect for their freedom but rather as a requirement of the church herself, for whom the variety of charisms in the individual institutes represents a rich source of evangelical witness and pastoral activity.[21] Obviously, the just autonomy we are speaking about does not signify in any way a

17. "Quae in cann. 578–597, et 606 statuuntur, societatibus vitae apostolicae applicantur, salva tamen uniuscuiusque societatis natura societatibus vero, de quibus in can. 731, § 2, etiam cann. 598–602 applicantur."

18. It is in this sense that one should read the word *patrimony* in the final phrase of canon 586 §1 ("and can preserve whole and entire the patrimony described in Can. 578"), since the word *charism* is not used in the Code.

19. See CIC c. 586 §2.

20. CIC c. 594: "Institutum iuris dioecesani, firmo can. 586, permanet sub speciali cura Episcopi dioecesani."

21. In canon 586 §1 ("Singulis institutis iusta autonomia vitae, praesertim regiminis, agnoscitur . . ."), the use of the verb *agnoscitur* is significant. The formulation indicates that a just autonomy is not the fruit of a concession by canon law, but rather a natural right of each institute, which the legislator recognizes by the act of giving juridical approval to institutes of consecrated life and societies of apostolic life.

total independence from legitimate ecclesiastical authority—for example, that of the pope[22] or the diocesan bishop.[23]

Clearly, religious priests do not need to be unique in the way adolescents strive to differentiate themselves from their parents or other authority figures. Rather, within the same presbyterium, religious priests should bring the spiritual patrimony of their institute as a gift to the particular church. In order that a diocesan ordinary might fulfill his responsibility of "preserving and safeguarding" a "just autonomy" for religious, an autonomy that is aimed at "preserving the entire patrimony of the Institute," it is clear that the bishop must acknowledge and appreciate the respective charisms of religious institutes whose priests are members of the presbyterium.[24] This appreciation will condition the way the bishop inserts religious into the pastoral planning of the diocese.

A "Just Autonomy" in Mission?

Today the question of mission preoccupies many institutes of consecrated life. There is an effort to overcome a certain dichotomy, insofar as the mission is not something over and above one's consecration; rather, as *Vita Consecrata* affirms, what one does is, in the deepest sense, an essential element of one's special dedication to God (72). That same paragraph of the apostolic exhortation affirms, "It can therefore be said that a sense of mission is essential to every Institute, not only those dedicated to the active apostolic life, but also those dedicated to the contemplative life." Earlier in the document, John Paul II teaches that "it can be said that the sense of mission is at the very heart of every form of consecrated life" (25).

The history of the Catholic Church in the United States has been marked by its "parochial" character. For many Catholics, the word *parish* is practically synonymous with local church. Catholic colleges, monasteries, health care centers, retreat houses, and the like are

22. CIC c. 590 §1.
23. See CD 35, 4.
24. CIC c. 586 §1, §2; cf. c. 578.

seen as "extras," as tangential to "real" Catholic life.[25] The "parochi-alization" of ecclesial life has had a major impact on religious, especially Institutes with ordained members. As the number of diocesan clergy has declined and the number of Catholics increased, religious institutes have felt an ever-greater pressure to administer parishes. Even religious who are not ordained have been inserted into parochial ministry in significant numbers.[26]

The demographics of and pastoral pressures on the ordained ministry in the United States portend decades of more pressure on religious institutes of men to provide clergy for the maintenance of diocesan parishes. These pressures may blind both the ordinary and the religious to the fundamental question of the fidelity of the religious to the foundational charism of their institutes and its proper expression in ministry. These pressures further exacerbate an ambiguity within religious institutes regarding the founding charism in the face of historical and accelerating trends towards the "parochi-alization" of mission in the United States.

A pioneering study of religious life in the United States emphasized the exceptional role clarity of religious involved in ordained ministry as compared to all other religious in their study.[27] But the hypothesis employed by the researchers to explain the phenomenon was that the role clarity of religious priests likely came from their

---

25. Paul K. Hennessy, CFC, "The Parochialization of the Church and Consecrated Life," in *A Concert of Charisms: Ordained Ministry in Religious Life* (Mahwah, NJ: Paulist Press, 1997), 1.

26. The "co-opting" of religious for parochial ministry has been present throughout the history of the church in the United States. The first members of my own institute arrived in the United States in 1832 with the intention of cooperating in the first evangelization of Native Americans and the apostolate of preaching parish missions. The bishops, however, insisted that the Redemptorists assume parishes among the growing population of Catholic immigrants. In the minds of the European leaders of the congregation, the cooperation of the confreres in parishes raised serious questions about their fidelity to the charism of the congregation.

27. David Nygren, CM, and Miriam Ukeritis, CSJ, *The Future of Religious Orders in the United States: Transformation and Commitment* (Westport, CT: Praeger, 1993). An executive summary of their research can be found in *Origins* 22, no. 15 (September 24, 1992): 258–72; regarding role clarity of religious priests as compared to other religious, see p. 261.

role as ordained ministers, not from a fundamental clarity regarding their identity as religious.

Reducing the mission of an institute to the provision of validly ordained priests for parochial work without regard to a renewal of the institute's mission not only demeans fidelity to mission and charism that has been emphasized throughout the initial formation of religious. It also deadens creativity within the institute, as satisfaction, personal fulfillment, and role clarity are enhanced by the very behavior that is leading to decline in the institute. Young religious often become socialized into a parochial model of mission and ministry.[28]

Hence, it should be recognized that a diocesan bishop might be cooperating in the real infidelity of religious if their insertion into the diocesan pastoral plan requires them to sacrifice such essential elements of their charismatic identity as community life, a preferential choice for the poor, a partiality to extraordinary preaching (i.e., noneucharistic preaching, such as parish missions, retreats, novenas), etc. If a bishop knows little about the charism or proper mission of an institute, there will be a greater chance that the pastoral benefit to the particular church results in lasting damage to the religious institute.

The shortage of secular clergy in a particular church can influence the religious priests who remain in the diocese. These can be tempted to respond generously to the sacramental needs of the diocese by assuming new commitments that effectively imperil their charismatic identity. Even today, number 11 of *Mutuae Relationes* can provide a salutary corrective to an excessively pragmatic vision of religious priests in a diocese: "In this hour of cultural evolution and ecclesial renewal, therefore, it is necessary to preserve the identity of each institute so securely, that the danger of an ill-defined situation be avoided, lest religious, failing to give due consideration to the particular mode of action proper to their character, become part of the life of the Church in a vague and ambiguous way."

The Code of Canon Law attempts to preserve the charismatic integrity of a specific form of consecrated life by putting clear limits

---

28. Cf. Ted Keating, SM, "The Religious Priests in the United States Church," *Touchstone* 13, no. 3 (Spring 1998): 16.

on the possibility for pastoral service by members of contemplative institutes.[29] The particular church should recognize that its exigencies may provoke a conflict among all religious priests, who must struggle to discern a way to respond generously to the needs of the diocese and faithfully to the demands of the charismatic project of their institute.

Hence, while the Code reserves explicit protection only to religious of contemplative institutes, and while the internal governance of an institute is envisioned by canon 586 §1 as the principal beneficiary of "just autonomy," given that the object of just autonomy is the preservation of the patrimony of the institute, a bishop should not simply insert religious priests into parochial ministry without regard for the essential elements of the charism of their institutes. While the institution of exemption[30] is one means of ensuring this autonomy of life, it should be reiterated that all religious remain subject to the authority of the bishop in those matters which pertain to the *cura animarum*, public worship, and other works of the apostolate.[31]

However, respect for the "just autonomy" of the institutes of religious priests in his diocese will lead the ordinary to fulfill his "pastoral duty" by "fostering religious life and protecting it in conformity with its own definite characteristics" (MR 9c). This responsibility includes doing his best to understand the *patrimonium* of the institute and the way the charism should condition the pastoral service of religious priests in his diocese.

Conclusion

Without a system of mutual relations that is based on the principle of communion, there is the real possibility that other forms of rela-

29. "Instituta, quae integre ad contemplationem ordinantur, in Corpore Christi mystico praeclaram semper partem obtinent: Deo enim eximium laudis sacrificium offerunt, populum Dei uberrimis sanctitatis fructibus collustrant eumque exemplo movent necnon arcana fecunditate apostolica dilatant. Qua de causa, quantumvis actuosi apostolatus urgeat necessitas, sodales horum institutorum advocari nequeunt ut in variis ministeriis pastoralibus operam adiutricem praestent" (c. 674).

30. See c. 591

31. See c. 678 §6.

tionship will enter the church: that of a commercial corporation, a parliament of opposing interests, or the law of the jungle, where only the strongest survive.

The strength of the church is found in communion, which is the real source for projecting the mutual relations among the disciples of Jesus Christ. The magisterium and canonical disposition can favor a harmonious and fruitful collaboration among bishops and major superiors. But not all the problems presented by life are resolved by the application of norms. The search for the common good of the church, love, and sincerity, together with a lively sense of communion and an appreciation for creative dialogue will always provide the best help.[32]

32. Teodoro Bahíllo Ruiz, CMF, "Las relaciones entre obispos y religiosos en la Iglesia: Realidad y perspectivas a los XXX años de la *Mutuae Relationes*," *Estudios Eclesiásticos* 83, no. 327 (2008): 565.

## Chapter 2

Religious Priesthood: Formation in the Present, Formation for the Future

Katarina Schuth, OSF

Introduction

This chapter is concerned with formation of candidates for the priesthood in the religious life—as it exists in the present and how it might be adapted in the future. Three specific topics form the structure of the chapter: first, the numbers of those preparing for priesthood in religious life and the location, subject matter, and quality of their programs of study; second, changes in the content of the *Program of Priestly Formation* (*PPF*) relative to religious orders; and third, formation practices of religious orders in light of their distinctive ministries and charisms, in response to church directives, and in consideration of other circumstances that contribute to the nature of suitable formation for religious priesthood. A brief history of religious orders precedes the main focus of the chapter in order to illuminate how the past has continued to affect the development of religious formation. The information demonstrates the importance of the founding purposes of religious orders and recognizes the role that the charism of each plays (or should play) in preparing its priests now and for the future. As the theology of ministry evolved through the centuries, so too did the foundation for appropriate preparation for ministry, whether for religious or diocesan priesthood. These dimensions—history, founding purpose, and charism—highlight why religious formation of priests cannot and should not be the same as diocesan formation. Thus, it is valuable to recognize the relationship between the two forms and how the similarities and differences should be reflected in today's formation.

An (Exceedingly) Concise History of Religious Formation

Although historians have a great appreciation for detail, the focus of this chapter allows for only a few essentials about the history of formation for religious priesthood. This basic knowledge about past religious practices contributes significantly to a fuller understanding of the present. Over four hundred years elapsed between the Council of Trent's 1563 Decree on Seminaries and the Second Vatican Council's 1965 document on seminaries, *Optatam Totius*. The massive changes in the church and in society during those four centuries eclipse even the differences between religious and diocesan priesthood; even so, the origins of the distinctions between the two are important. When it comes to formation in men's religious orders, one of the foremost authorities on the history is John W. O'Malley, SJ. He provides an enlightening summary of the key moments in religious order formation for priesthood in the introduction to *Reason for the Hope: The Futures of Roman Catholic Theologates.*[1] He begins with the caveat that tracing the history is difficult because it is a "singularly neglected" topic and, moreover, distinctive practices among religious orders do not lend themselves to generalizations. The reasons for the differentiation among orders are related to the historical periods of their founding, to the distinctive lifestyles of each congregation, and to their particular ministries. From the little that is known, however, O'Malley makes it clear that "historically and canonically speaking, we are dealing with traditions that are significantly different from the seminary tradition properly so called."[2]

---

1. In *Reason for the Hope: The Futures of Roman Catholic Theologates*, by Katarina Schuth (Wilmington, DE: Michael Glazier, 1989), 29–45. See also John W. O'Malley, "Priesthood, Ministry, and Religious Life: Some Historical and Historiographical Considerations," *Theological Studies* 49 (1988).

2. O'Malley in Schuth, *Reason for the Hope*, 29.

Using examples mostly from the twelfth century onwards, O'Malley provides several illustrations of formation practices of major orders that should inform present decisions about formation. Earlier, the Rule of St. Benedict encouraged or at least permitted study among the monks, even though detailed information about their specific academic requirements is not comprehensive or readily available. Since, for the most part, these monks were focused on contemplation and not engaged in pastoral ministry as such, the approach of their studies corresponded to their situation. Their formation, in line with their charism, was holistic and took place entirely in the monastery. Different circumstances prevailed by the thirteenth century, when great universities had developed fully organized degree programs in theology and philosophy. These were utilized by Franciscans and Dominicans, but not often by secular and monastic priests. Shortly after these early adapters, other mendicant orders like Augustinians, Carmelites, and Servites joined in sending men to the universities for training, all of them exempt from direct episcopal supervision.[3]

The Society of Jesus, founded in 1540, followed the example of the mendicants relative to ministry training in universities and sent all of their younger members for study. Their expansive notion of ministry extended far beyond diocesan boundaries and required special formation for almost all forms of pastoral care and spiritual guidance necessary to meet the spiritual needs of persons beyond what was then known as Christendom. By the middle of the seventeenth century, O'Malley writes, "training programs for the so-called active orders had been fully articulated and correlated with their ministries."[4] Though diversity was present, the pattern of formation was similar—beginning with a novitiate and continuing with an academic program in close relationship with universities. In communities with both ordained and nonordained members, the particular course of studies was determined by their ministries.

In the United States, the founding of most novitiates and houses of study began only in the late eighteenth century; prior to that time, due to lack of trained personnel, formation often took place in Europe.

3. Ibid., 30–34.
4. Ibid., 33.

When religious and political upheavals in Europe interfered, the pattern changed, and soon after more of the growing religious orders established institutions for formation in the United States. O'Malley notes that even before that time, as early as 1834, Dominicans, and then in turn Vincentians and Benedictines, had founded institutions where they trained their own and diocesan candidates for the priesthood. Redemptorists opened their first house of studies in New York in 1849, followed by Franciscans in several states from coast to coast. Jesuits were first trained at Georgetown and by 1837 had established five sites where scholastics were taught philosophy and theology. From these beginnings to the early twentieth century, programs were improved and stabilized. Smaller orders opened houses of study sometimes associated with universities, especially the Catholic University of America (CUA) in Washington, DC. Most often, "the houses of study remained 'total institutions' fully staffed with their own professors and having students who rarely, if ever, set foot on the campuses at which they were matriculated."[5] This pattern persisted until after Vatican II.

During the period immediately following the close of the council, many religious orders ended the academic programs in their small houses of formation and joined one of two new institutions—Catholic Theological Union (CTU), founded in Chicago in 1968, and Washington Theological Union (WTU), founded in Washington, DC, in 1969.[6] These new corporations, which provided academic and pastoral formation, were headed by members of sponsoring religious orders who were responsible for governance and operation of the schools. Religious houses supplied personal and spiritual formation. Several other new arrangements brought together smaller numbers of schools, some of which were located near various other institutions, including seminaries of other denominations. In 1968, for purposes of accreditation and ecumenical cooperation, Catholic schools became affiliated with the Association of Theological Schools and subsequently introduced the master of divinity degree (MDiv) for seminarians, as well as degrees for lay students. The documents

5. Ibid., 37.
6. WTU school was originally named "Washington Theological Coalition"; it was first called "Union" in 1977.

of Vatican II (*Optatam Totius* and *Presbyterorum Ordinis*) were significant in determining the courses of study, and they became the
source for the document *Ratio Fundamentalis Institutionis Sacerdotalis* (A Basic Scheme for Priestly Training), issued in 1970 by the
Sacred Congregation for Catholic Education. The deliberations of
the Synod of Bishops held in Rome in 1967 led to the themes to be
included in the *Ratio* and were in accordance with *Optatam Totius*
and other conciliar documents. This scheme was to "be examined
and drawn up definitively, so as to serve as a norm for all Schemes
later to be made: its purpose being to preserve unity and at the same
time allow sound variety."[7] The document was sent to all episcopal
conferences, indicating its obligatory nature, but it distinguished the
differences between the principal points that were "essential and
therefore necessarily to be observed from what is not to be so
considered."[8] Bishops were to promulgate programs for their countries, using the rules the document took for itself "in the preparing
or revising a Scheme for Priestly Training: to omit nothing that
seemed useful; to add nothing superfluous; to lay down nothing that
was not universally valid; always to pay attention to modern conditions." Concerning number 2 of the General Rules, the document
stated: "The rules of a Scheme thus worked out are to be observed
in all the Seminaries for diocesan clergy, whether regional or national;
their particular adaptations will be determined by the competent
Bishops in the Rule of Life proper to each Seminary. Training Schemes
of religious institutes are also to be adapted to these rules, comparing
like with like."[9] The distinctiveness of preparing for priesthood as
a religious was specifically recognized. Resulting from the *Ratio* was
another important historical reality—that is, the publication in 1971
of the first of five editions of the *Program of Priestly Formation* by
the National Conference of Catholic Bishops. The details of these
five documents and how they dealt with differences between formation for religious and diocesan priests are considered in Part B.

7. "1970—*Ratio Fundamentalis Institutionis Sacerdotalis* Issued by the Sacred
Congregation for Catholic Education," http://www.claretianformation.com/1970
-ratio-fundamentalis-institutionis-sacerdotalis/.
8. Ibid.
9. Ibid.

A. Religious Order Seminarians: Their Numbers and the Nature and Location of Their Studies

Two of the major concerns of religious superiors are the numbers of religious order candidates and the focus of the programs where they study theology. The considerable decrease in the total number of students at the theology level over the past twenty-five years is becoming progressively more disturbing; for religious theologates, this phenomenon is exacerbated by the fact that the decline is accompanied by an increase in the proportion of religious order students studying in seminaries operated primarily for diocesan seminarians. Regardless of the setting where religious are enrolled, the focus of programs is on human and spiritual formation in community as well as academic and pastoral formation in the schools. The focus of these programs differs between the two types of schools: in theologates for religious order candidates, assumptions about their life and ministry are built into academic courses, pastoral placements, and religious lifestyle, which is not the case in diocesan seminaries.

1. Number of Religious Order Students and Where They Are Enrolled

One of the most striking and lamentable statistics is the drastic decrease in the number of religious order candidates for priesthood studying at the theology and pretheology levels. In 1967–68, when the Center for Applied Research in the Apostolate (CARA) began to record these data, the number was 3,283, higher than in any subsequent year. Ever since then, the number of candidates has been on a gradual decline, with occasional upturns followed by further decline. In the early 2000s, the number was consistently over 900, but fell after that, perhaps due in part to the effects of the clergy sexual abuse situation. The number as of 2016–17 was 757, less than one-fourth of what it was in 1967–68. By decade, the combined number of pretheology and theology religious students was as follows:

- In 1967–68, when CARA began to record these data, it was 3,283;
- in 1977–78, it was 1,506, less than half of the 1967–68 figure;

- in 1987–88, it was 1,167, a drop of over 300 from a decade earlier;

- in 1997–98, it was 771, the low point in thirty years of records up to that year;

- in 2007–08, it was 797, and since then has fallen or risen slightly each year; and

- in 2016–17, the most recent year data are available, it was 757, the lowest number since records began to be kept in 1967–68.

An important factor that affects the veracity of these data is the introduction of the pretheology program in 1980–81. Before that time, the number of those enrolled in theologates generally included only theologians, so the post-1980 numbers presented above are inflated in comparison to the pre-1980s numbers. Although religious order theologates have not enrolled a high proportion of pretheologians since 1980–81, some of them do, and diocesan seminaries enroll many of them.[10]

Adding to the concern about numbers is the fact that an increasing proportion of religious are enrolling in diocesan seminaries, 6 of which are operated by religious orders, but the remaining 24 are under diocesan control (see Appendix A). The percentages of religious who studied in schools for religious order candidates over the past three decades are as follows:

- In 1989–90, it was 71.8 percent;

- in 1994–95, it was 68.2 percent;

- in 1999–2000, it was 70.8 percent;

---

10. The data reported by CARA do not distinguish where pretheology students are enrolled. They are recorded according to the reports of individual schools. Some pretheology students may be enrolled in a college seminary and could include religious order candidates, but since our main concern here is with the number of theologians, those total numbers are accurate, as reported in Appendix A, "All Diocesan and Religious Order Students Enrolled in Pretheology and Theology according to Type of School from 1989–1990 to 2016–2017."

- in 2004–05, it was 66.0 percent; and
- in 2009–10, it was 63.4 percent.

After that, the percentage dropped below 60 percent:

- In 2014–15, it was 55.1 percent;
- in 2015–16, it was 53.3 percent; and
- in 2016–17, it was 50.7 percent.

The overall decline in the percentage of religious candidates studying at religious order schools is above 20 percent over three decades, from 71.8 in 1989–90 to 50.7 in 2016–17. Since in recent years fewer faculty in diocesan schools are members of religious orders, the concern of superiors and formation personnel is that the distinctive mission and lifestyle of religious will not be as deeply ingrained in religious candidates who attend seminaries intended predominantly for diocesan seminarians.

Moreover, during the three most recent years, the 6 diocesan seminaries operated by religious orders have enrolled a smaller proportion of religious order candidates. Two factors may explain the lower proportion:

- First, only 1 of the 6 schools enrolled as many as 20 religious order students, and that was Oblate School of Theology in Texas with exactly 20 in 2015–16. In 2009–10, 4 of the schools had 20 or more religious order students.
- Second, with the closure of WTU, which was subscribed to by many religious orders, those students now enrolled in CUA at the rate of 36, 37, and 37 in respective years from 2014–15 to 2016–17.

Shifting now to the proportion of religious order candidates studying in religious-run diocesan schools, from 1989–90 to the present, the highest percentage was in 1999–2000, when 48.1 percent were enrolled; the lowest (26.6 percent) was in 2016–17. Thus, most of the religious order students now studying in diocesan schools are in the 24 that have no operating relationship with religious congregations. Of these 24, 6 of them have at times enrolled 20 or more religious order students since 1989–90, and 5 of them consistently enroll that number (see Appendix B). On the whole, over the past three decades a lower proportion of religious students have been studying in religious order schools, either those operated primarily for religious candidates or those operated primarily for diocesan candidates, with some religious candidates also enrolled.

What reasons might religious congregations have for choosing the theologates they do?

- Those who favor one of the 9 religious order schools are likely to do so because of the orientation to and focus on religious life; 8 of these schools are operated mainly for their own orders; CTU enrolls students from many religious orders.

  Three of the 8 schools are Dominican, 2 Jesuit, and 1 each Franciscan, Holy Cross, and Benedictine. As expected, each enrolls seminarians of its own order, focuses on its charism and mission, and is staffed mainly by members of its own order; most of the schools also serve a few religious from other orders, as well as lay students.

  Only CTU was founded for the purpose of serving many different religious communities in the academic and pastoral preparation of religious order candidates for the ordained priesthood (WTU was also founded for this purpose, but it is no longer operating). It has also enrolled a large number of lay students. Many congregations choose CTU because of its mission and location, as well as its diverse and large religious order faculty.

- Those who choose diocesan seminaries may do so because of tradition and/or because of location or affinity. Many religious congregations have combined several of their provinces into one, which for some has resulted in the desire to relocate their formation program near their headquarters.

- Others have sought a new situation since the closing of WTU. Financial considerations also may be a factor, based on variation in cost and scholarship support. In some cases, changes in faculty and in philosophical preferences contribute to the decision.

2. The Nature of the Academic and Pastoral Curriculum in Theological Schools

Broadly speaking, religious order theologates follow the prescriptions of the *PPF* for all areas of formation and those of the Association of Theological Schools (ATS) for academic and pastoral requirements. The *PPF* mandates four years of theology in preparation for priesthood, while the ATS requires three years of full-time study to earn an MDiv degree of about 90 credits. The religious order schools require credit hours ranging from 90 to 123. Generally, students spend four years in the theologate; some may do an additional theology degree in the fourth year. Areas of study prescribed by the *PPF* are listed below, along with the number of courses, the average number of credits required by religious order and diocesan schools, and the differences between them (see Appendix C for details).

	PPF Courses	Ave. Credits Religious	Ave. Credits Diocesan	Difference Relig./Dioc.
Sacred Scripture	6	17.5	18.5	−1.0
Patristics/Church History	3	8.6	10.6	−2.0
Spirituality	2	1.6	3.6	−2.0
Systematic/ Dogmatic Theology	9	18.5	18.5	=
Sacraments/ Liturgy	4	9.3	13.7	−4.4
Moral Theology	4	11.8	12.1	−0.3
All Pastoral	12	23.5	25.7	−2.2
Pastoral Theology/ Ministry	(5)	(9.1)	(7–8)	
Homiletics	(2)	(5.7)	(5–6)	

Canon Law	(2)	(4.1)	(4–5)
Liturgical Practica	(3)	(4.6)	(4–5)
Field Education	unspecified	9.4	10.3	−0.9
Electives	unspecified	7.1	9.2	−2.1
	(Spanish is encouraged)		
Total		107.3	122.2	−14.9

The smaller average number of credits required by religious order schools (14.9 fewer, equal to about 5 courses) can be attributed to the fact that in addition to a mandatory philosophy program, religious order candidates will have completed from two to four years of formation in prenovitiate, novitiate, and pretheology studies, and most will enter with a bachelor's degree. Before entering theology schools, many of them will have taken courses in Scripture and spirituality, and, depending on the religious order, some other fields of study. Whatever the number of credits and length of program, religious superiors sometimes question whether the charisms and ministries of their orders are sufficiently addressed in the schools, but they are not as concerned with the number of credits required.

3. *Provision of Human and Spiritual Formation for Religious Candidates*

Usually, most of human and spiritual formation is provided in houses of formation, where religious candidates live during their theologate years. Depending on the number of students, the staff size in these houses varies. Especially in smaller houses, several congregations may share resources and expertise to provide a well-rounded program. The schools also have some responsibility for human and spiritual formation since these areas are to be integrated with academic and pastoral formation. In most cases, for example, Scripture, theology, and pastoral courses will have a spiritual dimension that incorporates aspects of prayer, homiletics, and sacraments. Pastoral courses and field placements will take into account the charisms and ministries of the particular congregation. To ensure a cohesive and comprehensive program, emphasis is given to achieving a working relationship between academic faculty and the staff in houses of formation. For the most part, this relationship is more developed in the schools run for and by religious orders, responding to the interest of religious superiors who place a high value on having their candidates absorb more fully the meaning of religious life.

B. The *Program of Priestly Formation* in Relation to Religious Orders

The second part of this chapter examines the five editions of the *Program of Priestly Formation (PPF)* from 1971 to 2005 relative to consideration given to religious. The extent to which interests of religious order schools are represented in the *PPF*s has changed over time. The most significant changes came after the first two editions of 1971 and 1976, both of which included an extensive separate section on religious. In the third edition of 1981, the religious superiors conceded that "religious and diocesan priests share an increasingly pluriform priesthood" (*PPF* III, p. 3) and so it contains no description of religious formation as in the first two editions, though it does include a short statement from the Conference of Major Superiors of Men (CMSM). The fourth edition of 1992 and the fifth edition of 2005 include a similar brief statement and a number of references to religious superiors. The details of these differences are described below.

1. The Program of Priestly Formation, *First Edition (1971) and Second Edition (1976)*

When the *PPF* was first issued in 1971 (*PPF* I), the document was to apply to all seminarians—diocesan and religious. The CMSM responded positively to the *PPF* with the condition that a special section on formation for religious priesthood would be included. The section, which was integrated into the first two editions, focused on the nature of religious life and the vows but not on the distinctiveness of the ministry of religious priests. The eight pages were labelled

"Outline of Part Four: The Religious Priest's Formation" and were virtually the same in both editions (see Appendix D).[11] The first edition's index is limited to the main topics, but the index in the second edition (*PPF* II) provides more detail about these topics.

The chapters of "Part Four" deal with five areas: the nature of religious life, community life, commitment to the counsels, early training (novitiate), and administration. The first chapter gives a brief overview of religious life in general and notes that the goals of formation are to understand religious life and to recognize the distinctive graces of each religious family. The chapter on community life describes how living in community contributes to the formation of the seminarian. The third chapter, on the evangelical counsels, explains how the commitment to the vows is to be "a sign and witness to something beyond the grace of baptism and different from the grace of Orders" (*PPF* I 382 and *PPF* II 527). The fourth chapter refers to areas of formation in novitiate training: prayer, initiative, responsibility, community experience, and academics. The last chapter identifies how religious seminaries are to be "governed, to a greater or lesser degree, by the constitutions and other legislation or directives of the religious institutions" (*PPF* I 394 and *PPF* II 539). In the last paragraph of this chapter, the CMSM acknowledges that they accept "the guidelines of the *PPF* of the NCCB in regard to seminary administration . . . except insofar as otherwise provided by the distinctive regulations of each religious order or congregation" (*PPF* I 396 and *PPF* II 541).

2. The Program of Priestly Formation, *Third Edition (1981)*

Just five years later, with the issuance of the 1981 third edition of the *PPF* (*PPF* III), the treatment of religious is significantly altered. Gone is the separate section on the formation of religious priests, dropped in favor of a short "Statement from the Conference of Major Superiors of Men" accepting the omission of the special section that was found in each of the first two editions (see Appendix E). John O'Malley quotes from the statement of the CMSM that accepts the likeness between religious and diocesan priests and the fact that their

11. Found in *PPF* I, pp. 83–90, and in *PPF* II, pp. 123–32.

needs for priestly formation as such do not differ: " 'Thus the CMSM adopts the program of priestly formation as the one program for all United States religious seminarians.' "[12] From then on, religious order theologates were subject to the oversight of bishops and the same papal visitations as diocesan seminaries. O'Malley concludes that this self-understanding by religious orders of their mission and ministry "seems to have been simply conceded by them, never challenged or systematically argued."[13] The *PPF* III CMSM statement changed the historical relationship between religious superiors and bishops and the nature of the oversight of bishops from that time until the present. In *PPF* III, only about a dozen references to religious life are indexed; they deal mostly with the endorsement of the *PPF*, various religious traditions, and administration but make no reference to programmatic differences.

3. *The* Program of Priestly Formation, *Fourth Edition (1992) and Fifth Edition (2005)*

The last two editions of the *PPF* include a somewhat different CMSM statement (see Appendix F). It expresses the importance of collaboration with the Bishops' Committee on Priestly Formation and acknowledges the inclusion in the document of sections on religious priesthood that reflect the charisms and spiritual traditions of religious institutes. As in the third edition statement, it also notes that the CMSM adopts the *PPF* while "preserving the rights and privileges granted religious in church law, especially regarding the religious and spiritual formation of their own candidates." The fourth edition (*PPF* IV) mentions the role of religious superiors in some forty-five paragraphs, many of which in the same paragraph address a similar role for bishops. A dozen of the items—such as those dealing with charisms, the nature and mission of religious orders, and regulation of the formation process by the individual institutes and societies—concern religious institutes only. In the fifth edition (*PPF* V), thirty-three paragraphs mention religious orders and of those, about a dozen again concern religious institutes only.

---

12. Quote from *PPF* III #3 in Schuth, *Reason for the Hope*, 44.
13. O'Malley in Schuth, *Reason for the Hope*, 45.

Clearly, the relationships, collaboration, and interaction between religious orders and other diocesan and ecclesial structures have changed through the years, from 1971, when religious institutes were given recognition for distinctive dimensions of formation for priesthood, to 2005, by which time the "pluriform" nature of religious and diocesan priesthood had become the standard. As the new sixth edition of the *PPF* is developed, how the similarities and differences between the two are expressed in the text and how the CMSM and religious orders are involved in the process will be of great consequence.

C. Areas for Theologates to Consider in the Formation of Religious Candidates

In light of the change since the 1970s toward focusing more on the commonality rather than the differences in the expression of priesthood in religious and diocesan ministry and life, the last part of this chapter raises several areas of uneasiness for provincials, religious seminary personnel, and other community leaders as they construct their formation programs wherever their candidates are studying. Some of these issues and concerns are ongoing, while others surfaced in relation to the Vatican visitations, especially during the most recent apostolic visitation of the American seminaries and houses of priestly formation. This last visitation began in 2005 and concluded with a report on December 15, 2008; it was designed to assess the moral and intellectual state of US seminaries.[14] In the years that followed the 2008 report, religious order seminary personnel have reviewed their individual reports and gathered as a group to shape a response that covers a variety of concerns, both their own and those expressed in the reports.

Some of the formational matters are of a procedural or practical nature: admission requirements, international students, correlation with houses of formation where students reside, and education with

14. The other notable recent visitation was announced in 1981 when the Holy See appointed Bishop John A. Marshall of the Diocese of Burlington, Vermont, to serve as apostolic visitor. The process took almost seven years and concluded with the final report to the pope on July 2, 1988.

lay students. Others relate to content and topical themes, such as the use of church documents in courses and in program development (Vatican II, consecrated life, etc.), consideration of the vows and charisms of participant orders, and distinctiveness of courses and pastoral formation in ways that show they are directed toward the future ministries of religious. The leaders of religious order schools noted that certain ways of implementing programs and accomplishing the goals of theological formation need to be distinctive for their candidates. When interacting with ecclesial bodies that have oversight of religious order schools, they provided a description of the entirety of their requirements and an explanation of the differences for religious and diocesan candidates. Moreover, in some instances they underscored their own interest in changing or improving practices, as identified below.

1. Admissions Processes and Sources of Students

In the Vatican visitation report, it appeared that understanding of admissions requirements by religious theologates was incomplete. Religious orders usually have stringent and well-defined admission standards for those entering their congregations for the first time, either as a postulant or a novice. When candidates are ready for theological studies, more testing may be desirable, but not always necessary or expected by the theologate. Depending on the extent of testing on entrance to the order and the number of years from admission to studies in theology, US candidates are sometimes required by their superiors to take more tests in order to gain knowledge about changes in the candidate between entrance and seeking admission to a theologate. Both the order and the candidate can become aware of areas of growth that occurred and take note of inappropriate behavior or incompetence that needs attention on the part of the candidate.

For international students, who are admitted in large numbers, additional testing in both intellectual and psychological areas, as well as in language competence, is necessary. Information garnered from the tests after they arrive in the United States provides a comprehensive and current assessment of the candidate and an opportunity to discuss expectations of the school and the community with him.

Religious leaders noted the importance of making accommodations in the choice of tests to be used with international students. These should include forms that are available in a language the student is more familiar with and that contain questions suitable to the culture from which the student is coming. The tests should help ascertain the student's intellectual competence and identify assistance he may need in adapting to new learning styles. For ease in transition, transcripts should be acquired prior to admission. Obviously, travel documents such as visas should be sought far in advance of the beginning of the academic year to allow for maximum success once the student arrives. Provision for thorough assessment of all students according to their circumstances is part of religious order protocol that needed more explanation for the visitation process.

2. Prerequisites in Philosophy and Other Fields

Before students begin theological studies, they must have a significant number of credits in philosophy, the number of which has increased in recent years. Since students acquire these credits in various forms and from different institutions during the pretheology stage, this aspect of their academic program has to be reviewed before they apply for admission to theology.

Pope St. John Paul II in *Pastores Dabo Vobis* advised that "the so-called 'human sciences' can be of considerable use, sciences such as sociology, psychology, education, economics and politics, and the science of social communication. Also in the precise field of the positive or descriptive sciences, these can help the future priest prolong the living 'contemporaneousness' of Christ."[15] Although these recommendations are not required according to the *PPF,* religious superiors are concerned about them, since the ministries of religious orders are provided in a wide variety of contexts and countries. Formation directors are urged to pay particular attention to courses suitable to the charism of the religious congregation and the locations where they minister.

15. John Paul II, *Pastores Dabo Vobis,* post-synodal apostolic exhortation (Vatican City: Libreria Editrice Vaticana, 1992), 52.

3. Spiritual Direction and Spiritual Practices

The visitation teams took special interest in who was serving as spiritual directors and the location where spiritual direction was made available—that is, in the community or at the school. One of the directives of the *PPF* is that spiritual direction is to be provided by priests. A widespread concern in many seminaries is the lack of availability of enough priests who are trained spiritual directors. This problem is less frequent in religious communities, since as part of their ministry many of their members are trained and experienced directors. However, in smaller houses of formation where fewer staff are likely to be present, the necessity of having someone available is usually managed by sharing personnel with other houses of formation. Since some Vatican visitator team members were unaware of or misunderstood the arrangements, the negative critique in this area was viewed by religious formators as unwarranted.

Similarly, some visitors had questions about the daily schedule, including prayer times, acts of piety, and other spiritual exercises that may or may not be required in community, but are sometimes supplemented in the school. It was not always apparent to visitors that most spiritual activities took place in the community and that therefore a "Rule of Life," as required for diocesan seminaries, was not warranted in the schools. In reviewing the relationship between religious houses of formation and the schools, both visitors and formators emphasized the importance of coordinating schedules between them.

4. Educating Laity with Seminarians

Lay ecclesial ministry students are more likely to be enrolled in religious order schools than in diocesan seminaries. According to the 2008 report of the Vatican visitation, this practice is not desirable, but religious order schools have articulated a clear rationale for the dual enrollment of priesthood candidates and lay students. They believe that it fulfills the goal of helping students understand each other so that when they enter ministry together, they are more prepared to collaborate. Religious schools also consider it part of their responsibility to contribute to the church by educating lay ecclesial ministers. They have developed significant programs of spiritual and human formation for laity and some courses and programs that are specifically dedicated to lay ministry. Religious leaders consider it beneficial to make known the value of educating lay students and seminarians together.

5. *Program Content and Related Issues and Concerns*

It is necessary to provide a clear explanation of the particular requirements of preparing religious candidates for priesthood because aspects of their life and ministry are not identical to those of diocesan priests. Generally, religious are not parish-oriented, nor are they limited to a specified diocese or location. The history and founding purposes of religious orders help define the content of education for religious priesthood. The importance of the vows in religious life requires education that permeates all areas of formation. The charisms of various orders and congregations also warrant a different approach to pastoral formation. Sometimes courses are required to prepare candidates for future specialized ministries of the order, so pastoral placements need to reflect the same reality. The extent to which parish ministry is included in field education depends on the ministries of each congregation. Some are committed to parochial ministry in the United States, and many others are preparing international students who, as future priests, will be working in parishes. Other orders are more likely to focus on education, or preaching in the context of retreats and missions, or hospital and prison ministry. Regardless of where and in what contexts religious priests minister, their formation must be directed toward preparing them for those ministries.

Religious leaders are attentive to several other areas related to formation, including program focus, summer activities, and ongoing formation. On the whole, priesthood candidates are expected to be thoroughly acquainted with the documents of Vatican II, which are to be incorporated into all areas of formation. Religious candidates live in community during formation, and their required summer activities are specified by congregational policies; thus it is not within the purview of the religious schools to prescribe summer programs. Since this pattern is unlike that of most diocesan seminaries, the Vatican visitors were unaware of the difference and were in need of an explanation of the practice.

Several other areas were of concern. The drop in the number of faculty members who are religious is pronounced, so religious leaders need to be attentive to planning for educational opportunities to prepare more members to teach. Religious also need to receive ongoing education to be able to engage in formation ministry of future members. A final concern related to the reasons for differences in governance of religious order schools, which may have more than one provincial in the lead position, as compared to diocesan seminaries where one bishop fulfills that role. These are among the varied topics that religious leaders consider essential for the wellbeing of their orders.

Conclusion

This chapter has been concerned with the state of religious theologates, including the number of students enrolled in them, what and where they are studying, the relationship between ecclesial bodies and religious orders as identified in the *PPF* and Vatican visitations, and areas of concern regarding theological education in the future. Following a brief history of religious formation, the chapter described in detail changes in the number of religious order candidates. The decline has been steady since 1967–68, dropping from 3,283 to 757 in 2016–17; since 1990–91, the decline has been precipitous. Changes in areas of study have been gradual, with emphasis in recent years on maintaining the prominent position of Vatican II documents. Responding to the ministerial focuses of religious orders, some religious provincials, formators, and faculty are concerned about the type of theologate in which their candidates are enrolled. In 1989–90, over 70 percent of them attended religious order schools, it was barely 50 percent in 2016–17. The uneasiness about this pattern pertains to the possible diminishment in the extent to which candidates studying in diocesan seminaries are immersed in the knowledge and experience of religious life.

The relationship of religious orders with ecclesial bodies, including visitations of formation programs and the input they have into documents regulating priestly formation, especially the *PPF*, has changed through the years. Many religious leaders sensed that recent Vatican visitators were not well acquainted with the distinctive emphases and concerns of religious formation and therefore sometimes misjudged a situation. Through the years the distinctiveness of the content and focus of the *PPF* as related to the experience of religious formation has lessened. The first two editions of the *PPF* incorporated a significant section of "The Religious Priest's Formation," while the latest three editions included only a brief statement from the CMSM about their acceptance of the similarity of religious and diocesan priesthood as expressed in the document, with brief acknowledgment of some differences in "priestly life and work." Many religious superiors believe that the consequences of that shift need further clarification and discussion. Finally, the last part of this chapter identifies a series of procedural and practical concerns, as well as some content and topical themes, that need discussion among religious and with other ecclesial bodies. This summary leads to some questions about the importance of these findings:

1. How can the nature and purpose of formation for religious priesthood and its differentiation from diocesan formation be better understood and appreciated?

2. In what ways can religious leaders inform the principal authors of the sixth edition of the *PPF* about the structure and composition of the document so as to be aware of its impact on religious formation?

3. What do religious orders/congregations need to do together to plan and develop their formation programs to serve the future life and ministry of their members?

Appendix A

All Diocesan and Religious Order Students Enrolled in Pretheology and Theology according to Type of School from 1989–1990 to 2016–2017

Type of School	Religious Students		Diocesan Students		Total Students		No. of Schools
2016–2017							
In Religious Order Schools	328	(50.7%)	5	(0.2%)	333	(10.8%)	9
In Diocesan Schools	319	(49.3%)	2,434	(99.8%)	2,753	(89.2%)	30
# and % in Theology	647	(100.0%)	2,439	(100.0%)	3,086	(100.0%)	**39**
# and % in Pretheology (Type of school unknown)	110	(14.5%)	195	(7.4%)	305	(9.0%)	
TOTAL STUDENTS	**757**	(22.3%)	**2,634**	(77.7%)	**3,391**	(100.0%)	
Note: Number of schools with no religious order students: 4 of 39 (10.3%)							

Type of School	Religious Students		Diocesan Students		Total Students		No. of Schools
2015–2016							
In Religious Order Schools	359	(53.3%)	5	(0.2%)	364	(11.5%)	9
In Diocesan Schools	314	(46.7%)	2,487	(99.8%)	2,801	(88.5%)	30
# and % in Theology	673	(100.0%)	2,492	(100.0%)	3,165	(100.0%)	**39**
# and % in Pretheology (Type of school unknown)	139	(17.1%)	202	(7.5%)	341	(9.7%)	
TOTAL STUDENTS	**812**	(23.2%)	**2,694**	(76.8%)	**3,506**	(100.0%)	
Note: Number of schools with no religious order students: 5 of 39 (12.8%)							

Type of School	Religious Students		Diocesan Students		Total Students		No. of Schools
2014–2015 In Religious Order Schools	391	(55.1%)	4	(0.2%)	395	(12.0%)	9
In Diocesan Schools	319	(44.9%)	2,565	(99.8%)	2,884	(88.0%)	30
# and % in Theology	710	(100.0%)	2,569	(100.0%)	3,279	(100.0%)	39
# and % in Pretheology (Type of school unknown)	141	(16.6%)	216	(7.8%)	357	(9.8%)	
TOTAL STUDENTS	851	(23.4%)	2,785	(76.6%)	3,636	(100.0%)	

Note: Number of schools with no religious order students: 5 of 39 (12.8%)

Type of School	Religious Students		Diocesan Students		Total Students		No. of Schools
2009–2010 In Religious Order Schools	465	(63.4%)	2	(0.1%)	467	(14.8%)	11
In Diocesan Schools	268	(36.6%)	2,427	(99.9%)	2,429	(76.8%)	32
# and % in Theology	733	(100.0%)	2,429	(100.0%)	3,162	(100.0%)	43
# and % in Pretheology (Type of school unknown)	81	(10.0%)	213	(8.1%)	294	(8.5%)	
TOTAL STUDENTS	814	(23.6%)	2,642	(76.4%)	3,456	(100.0%)	

Note: Number of schools with no religious order students: 7 of 43 (16.3%)

Type of School	Religious Students		Diocesan Students		Total Students		No. of Schools
2004–2005							
In Religious Order Schools	543	(66.0%)	4	(0.2%)	547	(9.1%)	11
In Diocesan Schools	280	(34.0%)	2,179	(99.8%)	2,459	(81.8%)	33
# and % in Theology	823	(100.0%)	2,183	(100.0%)	3,006	(100.0%)	**44**
# and % in Pretheology (Type of school unknown)	161	(16.4%)	113	(4.9%)	274	(8.4%)	
TOTAL STUDENTS	**984**	(30.0%)	**2,296**	(70.0%)	**3,280**	(100.0%)	
Note: Number of schools with no religious order students: 8 of 44 (18.2%)							

Type of School	Religious Students		Diocesan Students		Total Students		No. of Schools
1999–2000							
In Religious Order Schools	575	(70.8%)	25	(1.0%)	600	(18.7%)	11
In Diocesan Schools	237	(29.2%)	2,375	(99.0%)	2,612	(81.3%)	33
# and % in Theology	812	(100.0%)	2,400	(100.0%)	3,212	(100.0%)	**44**
# and % in Pretheology (Type of school unknown)	83	(9.3%)	127	(5.0%)	210	(6.1%)	
TOTAL STUDENTS	**895**	(26.2%)	**2,527**	(73.8%)	**3,422**	(100.0%)	
Note: Number of schools with no religious order students: 10 of 44 (22.7%)							

Type of School	Religious Students		Diocesan Students		Total Students		No. of Schools
1994–1995 In Religious Order Schools	490	(68.2%)	16	(0.7%)	506	(17.0%)	12
In Diocesan Schools	229	(31.8%)	2,235	(99.3%)	2,464	(83.0%)	33
# and % in Theology	719	(100.0%)	2,251	(100.0%)	2,970	(100.0%)	45
# and % in Pretheology (Type of school unknown)	200	(21.8%)	145	(6.1%)	345	(10.4%)	
TOTAL STUDENTS	919	(27.7%)	2,396	(72.3%)	3,315	(100.0%)	
Note: Number of schools with no religious order students: 19 of 45 (42.2%)							

Type of School	Religious Students		Diocesan Students		Total Students		No. of Schools
1989–1990 In Religious Order Schools	658	(71.8%)	45	(1.7%)	703	(20.0%)	13
In Diocesan Schools	258	(28.2%)	2,560	(98.3%)	2,818	(80.0%)	35
# and % in Theology	916	(100.0%)	2,605	(100.0%)	3,521	(100.0%)	48
# and % in Pretheology (Type of school unknown)	205	(18.3%)	64	(2.4%)	269	(7.1%)	
TOTAL STUDENTS	1,121	(29.6%)	2,669	(70.4%)	3,790	(100.0%)	
Note: Number of schools with no religious order students: 15 of 48 (34.9%)							

Appendix B

1. Number of Religious Order Students Studying in Diocesan Schools Operated by Religious Orders

School ＼ Year	2016–2017	2015–2016	2014–2015	2009–2010	2004–2005	1999–2000	1994–1995	1989–1990
Holy Apostles, CT	9	11	16	**23**	**25**	**29**	**41**	**23**
St. Meinrad, IN	19	15	10	9	11	10	8	10
Mt. Angel, OR	13	11	12	**27**	9	17	7	10
St. Vincent, PA	17	19	16	**20**	15	**23**	12	16
Oblate, TX	19	**20**	16	**33**	**28**	**31**	**23**	**24**
Sacred Heart, WI	8	8	16	8	**24**	4	18	18
TOTAL	85	84	86	120	112	114	109	101
PERCENT	13.1%	12.5%	12.1%	16.4%	13.6%	14.0%	15.9%	11.9%

Note: Numbers in bold represent schools with 20 or more religious order students enrolled.

2. Number of Religious Order Students Studying in Diocesan Schools Operated by Dioceses with 20+ Religious Order Students

School \ Year	2016–2017	2015–2016	2014–2015	2009–2010	2004–2005	1999–2000	1994–1995	1989–1990
St. John's, CA	2	2	4	6	**22**	7	12	4
Catholic Univ. of America (CUA)	**58***	**58***	**57***	**21**	**36**	13	14	**24**
Notre Dame, LA	11	14	13	17	**22**	**22**	**20**	**23**
St. John's, MA	**39**	**36**	**34**	10	17	11	**26**	**38**
Immaculate Conception, NJ	**40**	**37**	**30**	**35**	15	**25**	**21**	14
St. Joseph's, NY	18	**20**	**21**	17	13	9	0	2
TOTAL	168	167	159	106	125	87	93	105
PERCENT	26.0%	24.8%	22.4%	14.5%	15.2%	10.7%	13.6%	12.4%

Note: Numbers in bold represent schools with 20 or more religious order students operated by dioceses.

*Significant increase in CUA religious order students is likely due to the closing of WTU.

3. *Number and Percent of All Religious Order Students in Diocesan Seminaries*

Year	2016–2017	2015–2016	2014–2015	2009–2010	2004–2005	1999–2000	1994–1995	1989–1990
All Religious Order Students	319**	314**	319**	268	280	237	229	258
PERCENT	49.3%	46.7%	44.9%	36.6%	34.0%	29.2%	31.8%	28.2%

Note: The sum of the totals of charts 1 and 2 is less than the number of all religious order students in diocesan seminaries given in this chart since the total of chart 2 includes only schools with 20 or more religious order students. The greater total of all religious order students given in this chart also includes those enrolled in diocesan seminaries with fewer than 20 religious order students.
**Significant increase in religious students enrolled in diocesan seminaries, including CUA, is likely due to the closing of WTU.

Appendix C

Comparison of MDiv Curricular Requirements: Religious Schools (2016–2017) with Diocesan Seminaries (2013–2015) and with PPF Fifth Edition

Sacred Scripture

Religious Schools (17.5 cr.)	Diocesan Schools (18.5 cr.)	*PPF* 5th Edition (7 areas of study)
• Intro to Bible/Intro to Old Testament/ Methodology of Old Testament (8) + Pentateuch (2) • Prophets (5) • Psalms and Wisdom Literature (5) • Synoptic Gospels (or Intro to New Testament) (7) • Pauline Literature (6) • Johannine Literature (6) (Additional courses or electives required by 5 schools)	• Intro to Bible/ Methodology of Old Testament/Old Testament Intro • Prophets • Psalms and Wisdom Literature • Synoptic Gospels/ Methodology of the New Testament • Pauline Literature • Johannine Literature	• Pentateuch • Historical Books, Prophetic and Wisdom Books (especially Psalms) • Synoptic Gospels and Acts • Pauline Literature • Johannine Literature • Catholic Epistles

Patristic Studies and Church History

Religious Schools (8.6 cr.)	Diocesan Schools (10.6 cr.)	PPF 5th Edition (3 areas of study)
• Patristics (3) + Ancient (1) • Church History I: Early/Medieval (7) • Church History II: Modern/ Contemporary (7) • American Catholic Church History (1) • Monastic Studies (1) (12 cr.)	• Patristics • Church History I: Early/Medieval • Church History II: Modern/ Contemporary • American Catholic Church History	• Patrology and Patristics • History of the Church Universal • History of the Catholic Church in the US (multicultural origins & ecumenical context)

Spirituality

Religious Schools (1.6 cr.)	Diocesan Schools (3.6 cr.)	PPF 5th Edition
• One course in Spirituality (2)	• One course in Spirituality • Nine seminaries require a course in spiritual direction	• Spirituality, including vocation • Spiritual Direction

Systematic/Dogmatic Theology

Religious Schools (27.8 cr.)	Diocesan Schools (32.2 cr.)	*PPF* 5th Edition (13 areas of study)
Systematic/ Dogmatic—18.5 cr. • Fundamental Theology (Method/ Intro) (9) • Ecclesiology (8) (1 of 8 includes Mariology) • Christology (8) • Trinity, God (7) • Theological or Christian Anthropology, Grace (6) (1 of 6 includes Eschatology) • Rule of St. Benedict (1) • Ecumenism (1) • Theology of Priesthood (4) • Elective courses in Systematics (9) • Religion and Society (1) (Elective courses [8 and 11] required by 2 schools in a variety of fields)	*Systematic/ Dogmatic—18.5 cr.* • Fundamental Theology • Ecclesiology • Christology • Trinity, God • Creation, Sin, Eschatology • Theological or Christian Anthropology, Grace • Nine seminaries require Ecumenism • Fourteen seminaries required Theology of Priesthood (Note below: seventeen seminaries require Holy Orders)	*Systematic/Dogmatic* • Fundamental Theology • Ecclesiology • Christology • Theology of God, One and Three • Creation, the Fall, the Nature of Sin, Redemption, Grace, and the Human Person • Eschatology • Mariology • Missiology • Ecumenism (and Interreligious Dialogue)

Systematic/Dogmatic Theology (cont.)

Religious Schools (27.8 cr.)	Diocesan Schools (32.2 cr.)	PPF 5th Edition (13 areas of study)
Sacramental/ Liturgical—9.3 cr. • Liturgical Theology (6) • Eucharist (4) • Sacraments of Initiation, Reconciliation, and Anointing (6) • Marriage (2) • Holy Orders (2) • Sacramental Theology (4) • Two elective courses in Sacraments (3)	*Sacramental/ Liturgical—13.7 cr.* • Liturgical Theology • Eucharist • Sacraments of Initiation, Reconciliation, and Anointing • Marriage • Seventeen seminaries require Holy Orders	*Sacramental/Liturgical* • Liturgy Core (theological, historical, spiritual, pastoral, and juridical) • Sacraments • Eucharist • Holy Orders

Moral Theology

Religious Schools (11.8 cr.)	Diocesan Schools (12.1 cr.)	PPF 5th Edition (4 areas of study)
• Fundamental Moral Principles/Theology (8) • Medical Ethics (2) • Social Ethics (6) • Choice of Medical/ Sexual/ Social Ethics (1) • Professional Ethics (2) • Two courses on Virtues (1)	• Fundamental Moral Principles/Theology (8) • Medical Ethics • Personal Morality/ Sexual Ethics • Social Ethics (Catholic Social Teaching)	• Fundamental Moral Theology • Medical-Moral Morality • Sexual Ethics • Social Ethics

Pastoral Studies

Religious Schools (23.5 cr.)	Diocesan Schools (25.7 cr.)	PPF 5th Edition (12 areas of study)
Pastoral Theology/ Skills—9.1 cr. • Pastoral Theology/ Ministry (6) • Pastoral Care and Counseling (6) • Catechetics (1)/ Adult Catechetics (1) • Parish Administration/ Ministry (3) • Intercultural Theology/Ministry (2) • Other and electives (4) • Monastic Formation (1) *Homiletics—5.7 cr.* • Beginning Homiletics (9) • Advanced Homiletics (7) • Homiletics III (3) *Canon Law—4.1 cr.* • Canon Law I: Introduction/ Marriage (9) • Canon Law: Sacraments (3)	*Pastoral Theology/Skills (7–8 cr.)* • Pastoral Theology • Pastoral Care and Counseling • Twenty-three seminaries require Catechetics • Half of seminaries require a course in teaching methods *Homiletics (5–6 cr.)* • Beginning Homiletics • Advanced Homiletics *Canon Law (4–5 cr.)* • Canon Law I: Introduction • Canon Law II: Sacraments	*Pastoral Theology/Skills* • Pastoral Theology: Principles and Criteria • Pastoral Counseling • Marriage and the Family (covered under Sacramental/ Liturgical) • Catechesis and Evangelization • Teaching Methods *Homiletics* • Homiletics • Bilingual Preaching (where appropriate) *Canon Law* • Introduction to Canon Law • Canon Law of Individual Sacraments

Pastoral Studies (cont.)

Religious Schools (23.5 cr.)	Diocesan Schools (25.7 cr.)	PPF 5th Edition (12 areas of study)
Liturgical Practica—4.6 cr. • Liturgical and Sacramental Practica (9) • Penance and Reconciliation Practica (6) • Deacon Practicum (3)	*Liturgical Practica (4–5 cr.)* • Liturgical and Sacramental Practicum • Penance and Reconciliation Practicum	*Liturgical Practica* • Eucharist • Sacrament of Penance • Other Sacraments

Field Education/Supervised Ministry

Religious Schools (9.4 cr.)	Diocesan Schools (10.3 cr.)	PPF 5th Edition
• Field Education (8) • CPE (2) • Pastoral Year (1)	• Field Education (9.5 cr.) —Education (required by thirteen seminaries) —Hospital/CPE (required by twenty seminaries) —Parish (required by twenty-five seminaries)	• Pastoral Experience • Theological Reflection

Electives/Other

Religious Schools (7.1 cr.)	Diocesan Schools (9.2 cr.)	*PPF* 5th Edition
• Integrative Seminar (3) • Comprehensive Exam for 0 cr. (1) • Synthesis (Seminar/ Exam) for 0 cr. (2) • Proseminar (1)	• Electives (7.8 cr.) • Integrative Seminar (2.0 cr.)	• Electives • Study of Spanish encouraged

Religious Order and Diocesan Schools: Difference in MDiv Requirements for Seminarians by Area of Study

		Religious Schools	Diocesan Schools		Difference
Scripture		17.5	18.5		-1.0
Historical		8.6	10.6		-2.0
Systematic		29.4	35.8		-6.4
	(18.5 Dogmatic)			(18.5 Dogmatic)	(=)
	(1.6 Spirituality)			(3.6 Spirituality)	(-2.0)
	(9.3 Sac./ Lit.)			(13.7 Sac./ Lit.)	(-4.4)
Moral		11.8	12.1		-0.3
Pastoral		23.5	25.7		-2.2
	(9.1 Pas. Th./Skills)			(7–10 Pas. Th./Skills)	
	(5.7 Homiletics)			(5–6 Homiletics)	
	(4.1 Canon Law)			(4–5 Canon Law)	
	(4.6 Lit. Practice)			(4–5 Lit. Practice)	
Field Ed/ Sup. Min.		9.4	10.3		-0.9
Electives/ Other		7.1	9.2		-2.1
		107.3	122.2		-14.9

Appendix D

The outline of topics on formation for religious priests covered in *PPF* I and *PPF* II is virtually identical and is as follows:

PART FOUR: The Religious Priest's Formation

CHAPTER ONE: NATURE OF RELIGIOUS LIFE
Article One: Religious Life in General
Article Two: Distinctive Religious Families

CHAPTER TWO: COMMUNITY LIFE

CHAPTER THREE: COMMITMENT TO THE COUNSELS
Article One: Evangelical Counsels
Article Two: Chastity
Article Three: Obedience
Article Four: Poverty

CHAPTER FOUR: EARLY TRAINING: NOVITIATE
Article One: Introduction
Article Two: Areas of Formation [in *PPF* II, these are listed A to E]
1. Prayer; 2. Initiative; 3. Responsibility;
4. Community Experience; 5. Academics

CHAPTER FIVE: ADMINISTRATION

Appendix E

Statement from the Conference of Major Superiors of Men: PPF *Third Edition, p. 3*

The Conference of Major Superiors of Men is strongly committed to ongoing close collaboration with the United States Bishops in the revision of the program of priestly formation. The omission of a special section dealing with religious in the present form of the program of priestly formation underlines the conviction that, while the priestly life and work of religious will differ from that of diocesan priests, the difference does not stem from their priesthood as such. Religious and diocesan priests share an increasingly pluriform priesthood; their needs for priestly formation as such do not differ.

At the same time, each religious community has its own foundational and renewal documents in which its distinctive charism is articulated, and for which no single section of a document on priestly formation in general can substitute.

Thus, the Conference of Major Superiors of Men adopts the program of priestly formation as the one program for all United States religious seminaries. They do this at the suggestion of the Sacred Congregation for Catholic Education and at the invitation of the National Conference of Catholic Bishops, preserving the rights and privileges granted religious in Church law, especially regarding the religious and spiritual formation of their own candidates.

Appendix F

Statement from the Conference of Major Superiors of Men: PPF *Fourth Edition, p. ii*

The Conference of Major Superiors of Men, recognizing its obligations to help ensure quality training and education for the ordained ministry, has over the past four years collaborated with the Bishops' Committee on Priestly Formation in revising the *Program of Priestly Formation*. We are especially pleased that the committee which drafted this revision of the document has seen fit to include sections dealing with ordained ministry within the context of religious life. Although academic requirements may be similar for both religious and diocesan priests, the religious priest will understand the ordained role and ministry as reflecting the charism and spiritual traditions of his religious institute.

The Conference of Major Superiors of Men adopts this *Program of Priestly Formation* as applicable to all religious seminaries in the United States. We do this at the invitations of the National Conference of Catholic Bishops, preserving the rights and privileges granted religious in church law, especially regarding the religious and spiritual formation of their own candidates.

Statement from the Conference of Major Superiors of Men: PPF *Fifth Edition, p. viii*

Same as *PPF* fourth edition except for minor changes as follows: line 3, change "four" to "few"; line 5, delete "especially"; line 6, change "has seen fit to include" to "has included"; and line 11, change "this" to "the" and line 12, add "Fifth Edition" after *"Program of Priestly Formation."*

Chapter 3

A *Program of Priestly Formation* for Religious Communities

Leslie J. Hoppe, OFM

The first edition of the *Program of Priestly Formation* (PPF) was issued by the National Conference of Catholic Bishops in 1971. It was a product of the collegiality and subsidiarity that reflected the importance of the local church in adapting Roman documents regarding seminary education.[1] The bishops invited representatives from the Conference of Major Superiors of Men (CMSM) to collaborate in the preparation of the *PPF*, and the membership of the CMSM accepted the bishops' document as a guide for the preparation of members of their religious communities for the ordained ministry. The bishops reviewed their *PPF* regularly and issued a series of four revisions of their original document. The fifth edition of the *PPF* was approved in 2005 and is the edition that is currently in force.

The thirty-five years between the appearance of the first and the fifth editions of the *PPF* witnessed profound changes in the seminary scene—especially for religious communities. Many religious communities closed their own theological seminaries. Some religious superiors sent their students to diocesan seminaries, while others sent their students to schools of theology that were staffed for and by religious. The "union model" for priestly preparation—in which several religious communities pooled their personnel and financial

1. The *Program of Priestly Formation* serves as the *Ratio Institutionis Sacerdotalis* for the United States.

resources, forming a school of theology and ministry for the priestly formation of their members—was another development. The two most notable unions were the Washington Theological Union in Silver Spring, Maryland, and the Catholic Theological Union in Chicago. Located in urban areas, near important universities and Protestant seminaries, these unions provided a new setting for Catholic theological education for ministry. Such education, which had previously taken place in isolated, rural areas, now took place in urban settings and in an ecumenical context.

The principal resources for the fifth edition of the *PPF* were the 1985 *Ratio Institutionis Sacerdotalis* issued by the Vatican's Congregation for Catholic Education and Pope St. John Paul II's 1992 apostolic exhortation *Pastores Dabo Vobis.* The horizon for both of these documents is the preparation of diocesan priests to serve in parochial ministry. The *PPF* reflects that horizon and envisions the preparation for priestly ministry as taking place in diocesan seminaries. Still, the CMSM remained committed to the bishops' *PPF,* stating that the CMSM "adopts the *Program of Priestly Formation* Fifth Edition as applicable to all religious seminaries in the United States."[2]

The fifth edition of the *PPF* was approved for a period of five years. It was anticipated that the United States Conference of Catholic Bishops (USCCB) would begin preparations for a sixth edition in 2010. During a meeting of the CMSM Formation Committee that year, a question arose concerning the participation of the CMSM in the work of preparing for a sixth edition. The committee considered a proposal to explore the possibility of a *PPF* by and for religious to be issued by the CMSM after an *approbatio* from the appropriate Roman dicasteries. After all, many religious prepare for priestly ministry in schools of theology and unions—not in seminaries as envisioned by the USCCB's *PPF.* The consequences of this were brought home during the 1981 and 2006 apostolic visitations of American seminaries. The teams that conducted the visitations expected to find seminary-type priestly formation and did not know what to make of the schools of theology and unions. Their forms of governance did not always reflect the model described in the *PPF.*

---

2. *Program of Priestly Formation, Fifth Edition* (Washington, DC: United States Conference of Catholic Bishops, 2005), n.p.

In addition, their student bodies were not made up only of men preparing for the ordained ministry but also included lay women and men preparing for a variety of ecclesial ministries.

There was some hesitancy on the part of several members of the CMSM Formation Committee about the prospect of preparing a *PPF* for religious. Some thought it a mistake to cut off this avenue of collaboration with the USCCB. They thought it necessary for the welfare of the church in the United States to maintain connections with the bishops' conference. In addition, some who had worked on the fifth edition of the *PPF* thought that this was too much of a project for religious to take on. The chair of the committee took an informal poll of several bishops, major superiors, and presidents of schools of theology to gauge their views on the proposal. Of the dozen individuals polled, only one had reservations about a *PPF* for religious. All the others thought it was an idea worth exploring.

The CMSM Formation Committee recognized the problems connected with the proposal for a *PPF* for religious. Some bishops might see the separate *PPF* as undermining the notion of the *one* priesthood in the church, believing that the one priesthood requires one pattern of priestly formation. There is also the perennial issue of the tension that exists between order and charism. These two difficulties, coupled with a move toward centralization on the part of the church's leadership, made securing permission for a separate *PPF* for religious unlikely. Nonetheless, the committee recommended that the leadership of the CMSM apprise the Congregation for Catholic Education and the Congregation for Institutes of Consecrated Life and Societies of Apostolic Life of the proposal. The officials at these Vatican dicasteries considered the proposal worth exploring but suggested that instead of a full-blown *PPF* for religious, the CMSM might wish to prepare a "compendium" as an appendix to be attached to the USCCB's *PPF*. The compendium would address the particular issues related to the preparation of men from religious communities for the ordained ministry.

Following the positive reaction of the two Vatican dicasteries, the CMSM appointed an advisory committee to explore the possibility of preparing a compendium for the sixth edition of the USCCB's *PPF*. The membership of the committee included Paul Bednarczyk, CSC (National Religious Vocation Conference), Justin Biase, OFM Conv (CMSM), Gary Riebe-Estrella, SVD (CMSM Formation

Committee, academic dean of CTU), Leslie Hoppe, OFM (chair, CMSM Formation Committee), Paul Liniger, OFM Conv (executive director of the CMSM), Richard Peddicord, OP (president of Aquinas Institute of Theology), Paul Philibert, OP (University of Notre Dame [retired]), James Schroeder, SCJ (Sacred Heart School of Theology), Katarina Schuth, OSF (University of St. Thomas), Donald Senior, CP (president, CTU), Fred Tillotson, O Carm (president, WTU), and Freddy Washington, CSSp (pastor/formation director).

The first task of the committee was to prepare a statement that could provide the theological, educational, and pastoral basis for a compendium on the formation of religious for the ordained ministry that could be appended to the USCCB's *PPF.* The advisory committee asked Paul Philibert and Katarina Schuth to write the statement, taking into account the discussion of the entire advisory committee. Because of a generous grant given to the CMSM by the Holy Name Province of the Order of Friars Minor, it was possible to involve a wider group of religious in the project. The grant made possible a one-day consultation in Denver in October 2010 that brought together administrators and faculty of several schools of theology, provincial superiors, and members of the CMSM board of directors. This group discussed a preliminary draft of the statement prepared by Fr. Paul Philibert and Sr. Katarina Schuth. They also considered the question of the sustainability of schools of theology and the unions run by religious for candidates for the ordained ministry from religious communities. The participants in the consultation commended the advisory committee for their work and made helpful suggestions to improve the statement being prepared by the committee. The participants also voiced serious concerns about the sustainability of schools of theology for religious and about the number of religious communities that send their students to diocesan seminaries for their priestly formation.

Shortly after the 2010 consultation, it became clear that the USCCB was not ready to go ahead with the revision of the *PPF.*[3] Instead of

---

3. One reason for the delay was that responsibility for priestly formation was transferred from the Congregation for Catholic Education to the Congregation for the Clergy. The latter dicastery issued its *Ratio Fundamentalis Institutionis Sacerdotalis* on December 8, 2016. Following the release of that document,

beginning work on a sixth edition, the bishops sought an extension of the Vatican's *approbatio* of the fifth edition for another five years. The CMSM Advisory Committee, however, decided to continue their work of preparing a statement that addressed some of the issues related to the preparation of candidates from religious communities for the priesthood. What began as a proposal for a *PPF* for religious in the United States became a compendium about formation of religious men for ordination and then finally a statement about religious priesthood and priestly formation proper to members of religious communities to be issued by the CMSM to its membership.

The statement, titled *The Gift of Religious Priesthood: Formation for Presbyteral Ministry in Institutes of Religious Life*, was approved by the CMSM Board of Directors in August 2011 and sent on to the members of the CMSM.[4] The intended audience of the statement was primarily the religious institutes themselves, underscoring the responsibility of the major superiors for the priestly formation of members of their institutes. It can also be used as a resource by bishops who wish to understand the formation of religious for priestly ministry and by administrators, faculty, and boards of schools of theology and seminaries.

The statement is not a comprehensive theological or pastoral discussion of the priesthood, but the committee hoped that it would stimulate a more comprehensive analysis of priestly formation for religious. Also, it is not a direct response to the report on the apostolic visitation of seminaries and houses of formation that

---

the USCCB decided to begin the process for the production of the sixth edition of its *PPF.* Rev. Ralph O'Donnell, the executive director of the USCCB Committee on the Clergy, Consecrated Life and Vocations, is overseeing the sixth edition project. Only one religious (John Pavlik, OFM Cap, the executive director of the CMSM) been appointed to the committee working on the sixth edition.

4. Before the statement was considered by the CMSM board of directors, it was sent out of courtesy by John Pavlik, OFM Cap, the executive director of the CMSM, to Archbishop Robert Carlson, then chair of the USCCB's Committee on the Clergy, Consecrated Life and Vocations. Abp. Carlson asked that the statement not be issued because he thought that proposing an alternative path to priestly formation was not "suitable at the present time." The CMSM board decided to issue the statement to its membership.

was completed in 2008.[5] The statement begins by affirming "the essential unity of the presbyteral order" and stating that the CMSM had "traditionally supported" the *PPF* issued by the USCCB, but it notes that the primary perspective of the *PPF* centers on the parochial ministry of diocesan priests, so some adaptation by religious is necessary. The statement asserts that the ministry of religious priests is an expression of the charisms of their religious institutes and that priestly formation of religious needs to take this reality into account. This does not mean that religious disregard the basic policies and procedures connected with priestly formation. In fact, the statement lists necessary adjustments of the *PPF* in light of the charisms and mission of religious, asserting that religious follow the *PPF* but in a way that differs from the way a diocesan seminary follows it.

Religious come to the task of priestly formation with extensive experience. Religious orders were training members of their institutes for presbyteral ministry long before the Council of Trent mandated the diocesan seminary system in the sixteenth century. The presbyteral ministry of religious priests is in service of their institutes' charism and an expression of their apostolic mission, which extends beyond diocese and parish and serves the broader needs of the church in teaching; preaching; chaplaincies; publishing; missionary evangelization; ministries with and for the poor; advocacy for justice, peace, and the integrity of creation; and theological scholarship. The preparation of religious for priestly ministry, then, must take into account the charisms and mission of religious life—something that the USCCB's *PPF* does not aim to do.

The CMSM statement describes how schools of theology and ministry are better equipped to respond to the formational needs of religious preparing for the priesthood. The priestly formation of members of religious institutes is to be grounded not only on the

---

5. The final report of the apostolic visitation is available at http://www.usccb .org/beliefs-and-teachings/vocations/priesthood/priestly-formation/upload/Final -Seminary-Visitation-Report.pdf. The content and tone of the report suggest that those conducting the visitations of schools of theology preparing religious for the priesthood prefer a seminary-type formation program akin to those in diocesan seminaries.

theology and spirituality of the priesthood but also on the charism and mission of the various institutes of consecrated life. In addition to the *Ratio Fundamentalis* of the Congregation for the Clergy, other important resources for the priestly formation of religious are the Rule and Constitutions, the *ratio formationis,* and the *ratio studiorum* of their institutes. Major superiors have the right and responsibility to oversee the formation of their members for the ordained ministry. The statement urges major superiors to claim their freedom and exercise their right to oversee the priestly formation of the members of their institutes.

The USCCB has begun the process of preparing the sixth edition of its *PPF.* Unfortunately, the USCCB committee responsible for preparing the sixth edition of the *PPF* has no plans to include a compendium on the priestly formation of religious in the bishops' document.

The CMSM document *The Gift of Religious Priesthood: Formation for Presbyteral Ministry in Institutes of Religious Life* is available by contacting the CMSM Office, 8808 Cameron St., Silver Spring, MD 20910-4152.

## Chapter 4

A Charism Complete: Religious Brothers and Clerics Together for Christ's Mission

John Pavlik, OFM Cap

Bridging a gap between laity and clerics, brotherhood in consecrated life and societies of apostolic life fully embraces the charism of each institute and witnesses to unambiguous discipleship, whether in homogeneous institutes of brothers or in mixed institutes often canonically defined as clerical.

The most recent data gathered by the Center for Applied Research in the Apostolate (CARA) tells us that brothers in the US church numbered 4,119 in 2016, down slightly from 4,200 in 2015, trending in decline from 12,271 in 1965 as the Second Vatican Council met.[1] Given the small numbers (in the Vatican's 2014 report there are 55,314 brothers worldwide),[2] the question posed at the multiplication of the loaves and fishes may be applied: But what's that among so many?

What difference would it make if the vocation of brother disappeared from American ecclesial life? What might a reassertion of this vocation contribute to our common mission for Christ? How

---

1. Center for Applied Research in the Apostolate at Georgetown University, "United States Data over Time," cara.georgetown.edu/frequently-requested -church-statistics, 2016. This data is based on the Official Catholic Directory (OCD).

2. CARA, "World Data over Time," cara.georgetown.edu/frequently -requested-church-statistics, 2015. This data is based on the Vatican's Annu-arium Statisticum Ecclesiae released in 2017.

does the church view the vocation of brother? How do brothers see themselves? What obstacles frustrate the full realization of this vocation? What might brothers do to affirm their vocation? What might fraternal spirituality look like? And what positive role might brothers play in this era?

My Personal Context

Six years ago a colleague asked me what priorities I planned to address in accepting the role of executive director at the Conference of Major Superiors of Men (CMSM). Having served eighteen years in provincial administration, and having recently completed that service with two terms as a major superior of our institute, I immediately thought of two topics that kept me awake some nights: care for our aging members and welcoming of new members. We witnessed a great generation of men who labored to build up Catholic faith in sponsored institutions, especially between the post-World War II years and the aftermath of Vatican II. We also witnessed a stream of vocations become a trickle as religious life renewed itself and sought a recovery and reassertion of each institute's evangelical focus, which the Holy Spirit had inspired founders and first followers to adopt and boldly express. Many male religious have rediscovered their rich origins, and we need to confidently invite the latest generation of Catholic men to own that treasure.

A few months into my position at the CMSM, I revised my priorities slightly to include the following: the role of the brother within institutes; substantive life formation that would uphold and support a man in his desired calling; and the encouragement of a passionate expression of the longing for God that would convince men to choose these forms of life. These elements will inform the comments that follow.

Truth Telling

Because we focus here on the prime place of the vocation to religious life, it is appropriate that we direct attention to our brothers in our institutes and in our American church, who witness unambiguously to their evangelical life. We must, however, seek to tell the whole truth about the history of their lived vocation. The phrase "tell the truth" expresses my personal awareness of the currents or subcultures that might operate within any institute, which might work against or on behalf of vocations and which might be addressed to allow newness and health, hope and healing. I will directly address some of these concerns later in this chapter.

Church Support for Religious Life and Brotherhood

In the following citation, Pope Francis expresses unequivocally his anxiety that priesthood carries temptations to privilege that water down the Gospel. The pope's comments to seminarians at the Spanish College in Rome on April 1, 2017, state a fear found in practice, whether in religious life or in diocesan local churches, that discipleship suffers when the disciple allows careerism to dominate rather than developing a freeing immersion in the Gospel invitation to serve Christ strongly as a disciple taken up in the mission Jesus chooses:

> Do not settle for a worry-free, comfortable life with an unhealthy attachment to money and an ambitious heart yearning for honors. I'm telling you this as a brother, father, and friend. Please shun ecclesial careerism. It is a plague. Avoid it. Everything hinges on loving the Lord with all of one's heart, soul, mind, and strength (Mark 12:30). That is what determines whether a person will be able to say "yes" to Jesus or turn one's back on him like the rich young man in the Gospels did. You cannot settle for leading an orderly and comfortable life that lets you live without worry unless you feel the need to cultivate a spirit of poverty rooted in the heart of Christ. Priests must have an appropriate relationship with the world and earthly goods if they are to gain authentic freedom as children of God.[3]

Francis's admonition addresses religious institutes on the danger of one facet of clericalism that destroys common vision and commitment. These same anxieties complicate the relationship of religious men to one another and potentially compromise our commitment to the mission.

3. Quoted in Carol Glatz, "Pope Francis: An Orderly and Comfortable Life Is Not a Life for Christ," *Catholic News Service*, April 3, 2017.

At a general papal audience on February 22, 1995, Pope St. John Paul II instructed the faithful on "lay religious," and quoted *Perfectae Caritatis* (10) to teach that "the lay religious life . . . is a state for the profession of the evangelical counsels which is complete in itself."[4] He further taught the assembled faithful, whose dominant model of church was that of a pastor and the congregants, that commitment to the priestly ministry is not required by the consecration which is proper to the religious state, and therefore even without priestly ordination a religious may live his consecration to the full. The faithful would already know this fullness in the persons of religious women serving Christ valiantly. The commonly voiced question to male lay religious reads variously: "So why didn't you go all the way?" "You are just a brother?" "We need priests." In effect, John Paul II held that the vocation of a brother needs no further justification than the profession of evangelical life.

The Congregation for Consecrated Life and Societies of Apostolic Life issued the first Vatican document exclusively devoted to the brotherhood as an evangelical witness complete in itself on December 14, 2015: *Identity and Mission of the Religious Brother in the Church*. While the document had been promulgated on October 4, it was not released to the public until December, and copies were not available until after the New Year, with copies in English published by the Vatican Press quickly selling out.[5] The document, written largely by brothers about themselves, describes the brothers in positive, scriptural, and ecclesial images. It asserts that since the very first centuries of Christianity consecrated life has been lived predominantly by lay members and has given expression to the yearning of men and women to live the Gospel with the radicalism proposed to all followers of Jesus. "Brother," the document teaches, is

4. John Paul II, Papal Audience, February 22, 1995, ewtn.com/library /PAPALDOC/JP2F2295.htm.

5. Carol Glatz, "Vatican Releases Instruction on Identity, Mission of Religious Brothers," *Catholic News Service*, December 14, 2015. Subsequent to the release of the document, brothers reported to the CMSM their efforts to acquire copies in Rome or electronically; once copies were available at Vatican bookstores, brothers in Rome also reported that English translations of the document quickly sold out, prompting brothers meeting in a collaborative think tank to petition for permission to publish an English/Spanish edition in the United States.

the name traditionally given to the male lay religious in the church since the dawn of consecrated life. "Brother" describes a relationship with the rest of the faithful that embraces equality and interdependence even as it implies closeness and accessibility.

Sainted Brothers and What They Witness

Saint Benedict, the founder of Western monasticism, was a monk, not a priest, fully embracing a particular charism that has achieved status as one of Western Christianity's greatest treasures. However, by 1075, German Benedictine monasteries in Europe, in response to requests that monks pray for people and their deceased families, had become local communities or monasteries of priests who offered Masses. Blessed William, abbot of Hirschau, petitioned the pope to "introduce lay brothers" into German Benedictine Monasteries, since laymen at that time were engaged in the work of the monasteries but living outside of them without benefit of membership or of religious vows. The abbot's petition represented a restoration, not a novelty.[6]

In Montreal, St. André Bessette (1845–1937), a Holy Cross brother, welcomed a wide range of women, men, and children to a more vibrant faith. Quite literally, he welcomed thousands of persons seeking God. He became for many a model of a man dedicated to transcendence. Perhaps he is best known for fostering devotion to Canada's patron, St. Joseph. Few saints rival St. André's evangelical witness. Research begun at the CMSM during the Year of Consecrated Life uncovered 3,403 saints and blesseds among religious institutes of men, representing ninety-three separate institutes. Of the total number, 1,452 were religious brothers or hermits representing forty-nine separate institutes.[7] A few institutes count more brothers among their saints than priests, revealing that holiness for members truly resides in the baptismal commitment without compromise.

6. Michael Ott, "Blessed William of Hirschau," *The Catholic Encyclopedia* (New York: Robert Appleton, 1912), http://newadvent.org/cathen/15629b.htm.

7. Research conducted by Martha Novelly of the CMSM staff throughout the Year of Consecrated Life and posted on a CMSM website dedicated to the year: http://www.yearforconsecratedlife.com/saints--blesseds.html.

What Contemporary Brothers Believe about Themselves

Members of five pontifical religious institutes of brothers meeting in Rome in the summer of 2012 articulated the following regarding identity, mission, and self-investment. Their words speak with inspiration and conviction.[8]

Identity

"Religious brothers are a group of men with vows who strive to place themselves at the heart of the Church, and publicly commit themselves to believe in God's love, to live it, and to spread it. Brothers respond to the call of Jesus 'to love one another.'"

"It is essential for the Religious Brother to live in community to acquire the support necessary to achieve a deep relationship with Jesus and all his brothers and sisters, working together to build the Kingdom of God on earth, a kingdom of justice and peace, that all may be one, giving special attention to the poor who are most in need."

"Believing that the purpose of religious life is the pursuit of the perfect love of God and neighbor, brothers work together with the people of God to be agents of healing in the world, to be the human face of God and a human extension of the communal love of the Trinity, keeping alive the dangerous memory of Jesus who came to serve not to be served."

Mission

"Brothers are at their best when they possess a fundamental simplicity and closeness to the poor, to ordinary people, and when they demonstrate a rootedness in the world, favoring the least and the lost."

Self-Investment

"They [brothers] commit themselves to a life of brotherhood even though they are not always sure of where it will lead them."

---

8. Intercongregational Conference, "The Identity of the Religious Brother in the Church Today," Rome: October 1, 2012.

What Young Brothers Say about Their Vocation

In 2013, a select group of young De La Salle Christian Brothers met in the Philippines to discuss their vocation and their hopes for themselves and for the congregation. With realism based on their apostolic and fraternal life experiences, these men identified seven areas to address within their institute, and by extension, within the brothers' vocations in general.[9]

First, they discussed the need to have a vibrant association for educational services to the poor, because as committed as they remain to serving the poor, they realize they can only do so now in collaboration with their lay partners because the number of brothers has decreased. These men do not wish their rich charism to flounder now that the number of men chiefly possessing or carrying that charism has diminished. To say this more positively, these men accept collaboration with other laity as a fundamental value, so they realize the need to pass on the charism to laity even as they themselves become stronger in the assertion of their charism.

Secondly, they commit to service to the poor as a primary expression of their charism; nevertheless, they accept that the number of poor persons is far too great for them to respond to all the poor they will identify. In one sense, they easily identify the periphery to which they are drawn and they acknowledge that the impulse towards offering Christ-like service to the poor remains as strong or as compelling as ever.

Thirdly, they affirm that a strong common life is essential for fulfilling the commitment they have made, but they know that they must balance prayer, ministry, and fraternal presence. These men know the reality of ministerial burnout and the isolation that individualism creates, destroying the bonds of brotherhood.

Fourthly, they are convinced that each brother must strive to be an interior man who is never neglectful of the spiritual dimensions of his personal and communal life.

Fifthly, these men agree that they must commit to rejoice in each new vocation and explicitly choose to accompany the new men joining

---

9. International Young Brothers Assembly, "Our Future Hopes and Dreams," Philippines: July 29–August 7, 2013.

them. Every new vocation joins the institute, and each professed member has something to contribute to fostering vocations.

Sixthly, with a background in contemporary education, these men believe that young people are still searching for spiritual meaning and gravitate to a call to serve others.

Finally, they acknowledge that they must be proficient in new means of communication through social media if they are to reach youth with the message of their charism.

Obstacles to the Fulfillment of the Brother's Vocation

The following observations may seem tough, but they are not without some basis in fact.

1. Tenuous charisms flounder. Everyone who acknowledges a vocation to be a brother must articulate his place within the foundational charism of the institute to which he belongs. If he cannot articulate his place, both he and the institute suffer.

2. Clericalism scourges. Scratch the surface seeking accounts of clericalism, and very quickly wounds bleed anew as men recount stories of clerics who arrogantly treated brothers as less than themselves, whether as members in the same institute or as men interacting with pastors. Cruelty is not too strong a term to describe the absence of charity experienced.

3. Lack of assertiveness enables. Choosing to appease or to avoid difficulty, brothers bear some blame for not asserting themselves as equal members of consecrated life or apostolic life. A false sense of humility, along with some excusing of sinfulness and dysfunctionality, has led to brothers bearing a good bit of pain from arrogance and pride.

4. Sexual abuse still wounds. The exposure of sexual abuse has opened the church and American society to close scrutiny. To label all abuse in the church as clerical misses identifying the enabling culture that allowed members not to see and name harmful and problematic behaviors. Brothers also violated the sacred trust people placed in church personnel, resulting in the devastating lack of trust that hobbles the evangelical spirit.

5. Ease of withdrawal offends. Although brothers speak of permanent commitment to a vocation rich in its spirituality and outreach, they have voiced surprise and dismay about how easily a man in permanent commitment can withdraw from the institute without repercussions, as if the church takes their commitment less seriously than that of priests. Are permanent commitments more permanent for people in sacred orders or in matrimony than for men and women in religious vows?

6. Institutions collapse. Brothers worked diligently to build up the body of believers and identified with secondary schools or colleges, hospitals, and other facilities. Diminishment touches institutions, too, and brothers grieve the loss of what so inspired them that they poured out their life blood for these good works.

7. Age fatigues. With a large percentage of their members in retirement or in illness, brothers have less hope about their future. As they age, brothers wear out and see little to give them new strength.

8. Lack of jurisdiction smarts. The debate within "mixed institutes" has now raged for forty years without achieving a clear change in canon law that would permit a brother to exercise jurisdiction over a priest-peer in his institute, regardless of the aptitude of the brother for the exercise of fraternal care. We may speak all we wish about the equality of membership, but this failure to resolve a burning question within spiritual families where founders clearly permitted and encouraged sharing the burden of office offends, and may offend deeply.

These eight issues cry out for resolution if the vocation of brother is to be recognized and affirmed publicly in the church.

Aspects of the Vocation of Brother That Appeal and Invite

Truth be told, the vocation of brother manages well to appeal to men today. This brief list of positive aspects of a brother's vocation hardly exhausts the attractive factors, but may offer a positive beginning to an inquiry about this form of discipleship.

1. Welcoming strangers and the estranged. The relationship of brothers to people often allows the person receiving them to minimize any distance rightly or wrongly perceived and associated with the clerical state. Or to describe this dynamic another way, the power exchange of pastor to congregant is not the same as that of a lay member of a religious institute to a lay man or woman. The relationship of lay-to-lay eases bonding.

2. Real power in the gifts. The brother has a set of identified gifts to share, and he offers them freely. His power does not depend upon office.

3. Transcendence appeals. Brothers accept and profess religious life because they are seeking God. Their direct pursuit appeals to other persons who may identify with them as more "ordinary" examples of discipleship.

4. Mission drives. Brothers with a well-developed sense of mission and with a singular devotion to its fulfillment accomplish good things and become attractive to others who wish to devote their lives to Christ's mission and to the service of humanity. Young people often express an interest in devoting themselves to doing good things for people in need.

5. Fraternity saves. Brothers living as brothers to one another not only affirm and support one another but also witness to how people may live with one another in a community not based on hierarchy or status.

6. Identification without distance heals. Brothers may readily identify with people on various peripheries in such a way as to respect, heal, and assist without immediately assuming another role to assert their position.

7. Connection to the underserved raises up. Because brothers often reach out to the most underserved in fields of education and health care, they find recognition for their sacrifice and have managed to assist generations of people in need.

Characteristics/Qualities That Support a Brother in His Vocation

In consultation with CMSM members, two young brothers in temporary profession serving internships at the CMSM national office, Benjamin Babb, SDS, and Nicholas Draggone, OFM Conv, consulted with brothers, both their peers and their elders, interviewing, surveying, and recording their opinions on various aspects of their vocations. Not a formal, disciplined study, these unpublished consultations reported personal, anecdotal experiences over a lifetime of commitment. The information and experiences the brothers shared revealed that they desire a developed spirituality of brotherhood that incorporates some of the following ideas:

- Fraternal spirituality should allow for the nurturing of fraternal, human relationships, asking where the brother finds Christ in those he encounters. *Jesus is brother to all.*

- This spirituality should embrace the world with joy and recognize it as a sacred space where brothers can expect to promote genuine human relationships. *Jesus came to save the world, not to condemn it.*

- This spirituality should help brothers to be close to the experience of ordinary people and to manifest respect and reverence for religious values in all nations, races, and peoples. *Jesus ate and drank with sinners and sent disciples out to encounter all persons.*

In *Vita Consecrata*, Pope John Paul II developed five aspects of the spirituality of brothers, very briefly stated as these: brothers of and to Christ; brothers to one another; brothers universally to every man, woman, and child; brothers for a greater sense of brotherhood in the church; and brothers in total self-giving to Christ and to the people.[10]

---

10. John Paul II, *Vita Consecrata*, post-synodal apostolic exhortation (Vatican City: Libreria Editrice Vaticana, 1996), "Religious Brothers," 60.

What the Vocation of Brother Offers to the World Today

In conclusion, the 2015 Vatican-issued *Identity and Mission of the Religious Brother in the Church* proposes that every era needs prophets, and it suggests that brothers might accept that role for this era (37). The text suggests five ways for brothers to adopt this role: as prophets of hospitality with openness and acceptance towards strangers and foreigners in the face of intolerance and exclusion; as prophets of the meaning of life, pointing to what is essential; as prophets affirming the feminine values in the history of humanity, thus opening new horizons for evangelization; as prophets of care and protection of life and of the integrity of creation; and as prophets of the wise use of new technologies at the service of communication and education, especially for the disadvantaged.

The vocation of brother ought to be presented assertively to the church today as a way of living out the baptismal call of all believers and as a way of life that truly makes a difference by building up all in the true love of God for the world.

## Chapter 5

A Theologian's Perspective on Priesthood in Religious Life

Edward P. Hahnenberg, PhD

I was invited to address priesthood in religious life from the perspective of a theologian. This is a good thing, because I cannot do so either from the vantage point of a priest or from the experience of religious life.

What follows, therefore, is a series of theological observations that I hope will provide some context and rationale for the other contributions to this volume. These theological observations are meant to invite reflection on our contemporary, postconciliar period in light of the long history of reflection on Christian ministry. In making these observations, I do not intend to suggest an overarching theological paradigm into which I expect everything to fit. Indeed, what I hope you will see is that I am much more interested in what does *not* fit. If there is a thesis in what follows, it is one that comes from Pope Francis: Realities are more important than ideas. Experiences are more important than words.

Searching for a Comprehensive Theology of Ministry

Allow me to offer a bit of personal background. I completed my PhD at the University of Notre Dame in 2002, with a dissertation on "The Emergence and Sources of Lay Ecclesial Ministry." At the time, I was interested not only in the historical unfolding of this ministerial reality, but also in the developing ways the reality was treated theologically. In my attempt to construct a contemporary theology of ministry, one of the things that frustrated me was a lack of dialogue between what seemed to be two separate conversations going on within the postconciliar literature.

On the one hand, there was the conversation surrounding lay ministry that was taking place among theologians within universities, ministry formation programs, and national ministry associations. This conversation was heavily pneumatological and functional. It emphasized the charisms of the Spirit emerging "from below," flowing out of baptism and toward an individual's ministry.

On the other hand, there was the conversation surrounding priesthood that was taking place within seminaries, bishops' committees, and Vatican offices. This conversation was heavily christological and ontological. It stressed the gift of God that comes "from above" through ordination, the power to act "in the person of Christ" and represent Christ to the community.

It seemed that one had to choose between a "low" theology of ministry that failed to address priestly identity and a "high" theology of ministry that failed to incorporate the many new ministries emerging in our church. As a systematic theologian, I was looking for a more comprehensive vision, a more holistic theology. And I thought that I had found it in an integrated, systematic theology of ministry that drew together the entire postconciliar conversation—uniting the christological and the pneumatological, the ontological and the functional, institution and charism, ordination and baptism, "from above" and "from below," church and world, heaven and earth—all within a thoroughly relational appeal to the doctrine of the Trinity.[1]

And it was beautiful. A comprehensive theology of ministry into which everything fit.

Then I stumbled across a 1988 essay by the Jesuit historian John O'Malley, titled "Priesthood, Ministry, and Religious Life: Some Historical and Historiographical Considerations"—which, I am embarrassed to admit, was already fifteen years old when I discovered it, and whose basic argument was repeated in several essays during

---

1. Edward P. Hahnenberg, *Ministries: A Relational Approach* (New York: Crossroad, 2003).

the 1990s.[2] Ever since, I have been much less interested in making things fit into a comprehensive system, than I have been interested in exploring what does not fit.

One Priesthood, Two Traditions

O'Malley's essay begins with the Second Vatican Council's teaching on the priesthood. He welcomes the council's emphasis on the *ministry* of the priest, which he sees as a helpful corrective to the magisterium's previous emphasis on the *status* or ontology of priesthood. According to Vatican II, priesthood is first and foremost a ministry— it is service done for others in the person of Christ. But O'Malley asks: What is the precise nature of this ministry? According to Vatican II, O'Malley argues, the ministry of the priest is marked by three basic characteristics. It is a ministry (1) by and large to the Christian faithful; (2) conceived of as taking place within a stable community of faith; and (3) done in hierarchical union with the bishop.[3]

O'Malley points out that these three characteristics fit pretty well the ministry of diocesan priests. But they do not fit as well the ministry of religious priests—that is, priests living according to vows in a religious order or congregation. In fact, particularly in its emphasis on the priest's relationship to the bishop, the council's vision of priesthood actually *contradicts* the history, self-understanding, and

2. John W. O'Malley, "Priesthood, Ministry, and Religious Life: Some Historical and Historiographical Considerations," *Theological Studies* 49 (1988): 223–57. See also O'Malley, "Diocesan and Religious Models of Priestly Formation: Historical Perspectives," in *Priests: Identity and Ministry*, ed. Robert J. Wister (Wilmington, DE: Michael Glazier, 1990), 54–70; O'Malley, "Spiritual Formation for Ministry: Some Roman Catholic Traditions—Their Past and Present," in *Theological Education and Moral Formation*, ed. Richard John Neuhaus (Grand Rapids, MI: William B. Eerdmans, 1992), 79–111; O'Malley, "One Priesthood: Two Traditions," in *A Concert of Charisms: Ordained Ministry in Religious Life*, ed. Paul K. Hennessy (New York: Paulist, 1997), 9–24; O'Malley, "The Ministry to Outsiders: The Jesuits," in *A History of Pastoral Care*, ed. G. R. Evans (London: Cassell, 2000), 252–61; O'Malley, *The First Jesuits* (Cambridge, MA: Harvard University Press, 1993), 51–90.

3. O'Malley, "Priesthood, Ministry, and Religious Life," 224.

canonical structures of religious order priests—a ministerial reality that evolved within a tradition of explicit *exemption* from episcopal oversight. There is significant ministerial diversity here that Vatican II simply glosses over.

According to O'Malley, at the root of the problem is the way in which history is read. He argues that there is a fifteen-hundred-year blind spot in Catholic historical scholarship on ministry and priesthood and lays out several unexamined biases responsible for this rather significant oversight. These include the tendency to deal almost exclusively with the biblical and patristic periods, to the neglect of ministerial developments in the modern period; a focus on *ideas* about ministry found in past theologians or *ideals* of ministry found in official documents, rather than on what was actually happening "on the ground"; and an implicit assumption that Vatican II stands as the culmination of the historical evolution of ministry and the final criterion for assessing the life of the church, which, interestingly and paradoxically, forestalls the possibility of future, unforeseen developments.

Ministry That Is Patristic and Pastoral

The result of this historiographical trajectory is that the ministry of religious order priests does not seem to fit within the fundamental theological paradigm that guides the Catholic discussion of church order. If I were to name this paradigm concisely, I would call it a patristic and pastoral model of ministry.

To speak of a patristic model of ministry is to evoke that Golden Age of church order in the fourth, fifth, and sixth centuries. Very little is known about ministry before this period. What we do know suggests that those early years were a time of incredible flux and fluidity in ministerial forms. By the early second century, certain important roles took shape, but local diversity remained the norm, and offices continued to evolve. Over the course of the third century, a more stable situation started to emerge, as canon, creed, and community leadership began to offer greater consistency to the faith. By the fourth century, with the imperial recognition of the church, a familiar pattern centered on a few important ministries finally took hold. This was a time—after centuries of periodic persecution, but before the decline of the early medieval period—when brilliant bishops like Ambrose, Augustine, Gregory of Nazianzus, and John Chrysostom organized their churches, wrote rich theological treatises, and preached deeply moving sermons. In their carefully preserved writings, and in the various liturgical documents that have survived, we catch our best glimpse of ministerial order in the "early church." Here—in its classic patristic form— ministry revolved around a single bishop in each local church, a shepherd surrounded by his council of presbyters, deacons, and a host of other ministers serving the Christian community. This ministerial order was symbolized beautifully when the whole local church gathered around the bishop at the table of the eucharistic celebration—a liturgy that drew the horizontal communion of the church into vertical communion with the triune God.

This patristic conception of ministry survived as a powerful ideal over the course of Christian history, even if it was rarely, if ever, enacted in the concrete. As I want to suggest, it is a vision that continues to exercise a powerful hold on the Catholic ecclesiological imagination. It is, in fact, the fundamental vision of ministry presented in the documents of the Second Vatican Council. This is not coincidental. The documents of Vatican II were influenced by—even written by—twentieth-century theological giants of *ressourcement*, men like Yves Congar, Henri de Lubac, Joseph Ratzinger, and Jean Daniélou, who had dedicated their life's work to recovering the great riches of the Christian tradition. Of these riches, no period shone more brightly for these scholars than the Golden Age of the early church. This appreciation is reflected in the council documents, which hold up the ideal of the patristic church order as the fundamental framework for its discussion of ministry.

Ministry That is Modern and Missionary

And yet, a patristic and pastoral model is not the only shape ministry has taken. Ministry moved on after the sixth century. O'Malley's essay points to the incredible ministerial diversity that marked the time between the patristic and the present, in particular to two historical eras.

The first is the thirteenth century, during which time the kind of pervasive, grass-roots enthusiasm for the apostolic life that character-ized late medieval Europe burst forth into a new and lasting minis-terial form: the friars. With the friars—the most well known are the Dominicans and the Franciscans, but this movement also included the Carmelites, Augustinians, Servites, and many others—we find a new form of service emerging out of pastoral need and personal ex-perience. We see diversity in ministry.

For example, the Dominicans were founded to confront the Al-bigensians, a heretical movement that the ministerial structures of the day were simply incapable of responding to effectively. The structures in place were not working. Something new was needed. And specific ministerial forms took shape to meet specific needs. Good teaching and good preaching were in short supply, so the Do-minicans (the Order of Preachers) stressed education for their mem-bers. The opulence of the clergy was condemned by the Albigensians, so the vow of poverty was embraced, in part in order that the Do-minicans might get a hearing. Mobility was required to respond to a rapidly spreading movement, so the friars abandoned the monastery and successfully campaigned for freedom from the supervision of local bishops.

This last point—exemption from episcopal oversight—strikes O'Malley as a historian.[4] Earlier exemptions from episcopal oversight granted to monasteries like Cluny were meant to safeguard the in-ternal governance of those communities. The exemption granted to the Dominicans and the Franciscans was of a different sort. It was intended to protect not only the internal governance of these new orders, but also their ministry. In other words, the friars successfully argued that they had to be free from the control of the bishop in order to accomplish their ministry more effectively.

The second period O'Malley highlights is the sixteenth century. For O'Malley, who is himself a Jesuit, it is through the Society of Jesus that the experimentation and freedom in ministry initiated by the mendicants is taken to new heights. The early modern period, he argues, was not simply a reactionary time of Counter-Reformation.

---

4. Ibid., 236.

It was, in fact, one of the most explosive and expansive periods of ministerial innovation in the history of the church. It was a time of incredible creativity in ministry, a time when anything that seemed to produce fruit for the good of souls or for the mission of the church was pursued with energetic zeal and hard-headed pragmatism. We could say the same for the dozens and dozens of communities of active religious life founded since the sixteenth century—congregations of women marked by the same energetic creativity and ministerial flexibility.

In the mendicants, in the Jesuits, in the sisters, O'Malley concludes, we discover a history of ministerial adaptation that stands in marked contrast to the more "normative" approach to church order that dominates so much of our present ecclesial consciousness.[5] These new forms represent classic "exceptions" to the patristic vision of ministry. They evoke a different vision, a different model—not "patristic and pastoral," but what we might call "modern and missionary." The first (patristic and pastoral) emphasizes ministry to the Christian faithful, in a stable community, under the supervision of the bishop. The second (modern and missionary) is embodied in a priestly ministry oriented both to the faithful and to those outside the fold, one that moves beyond the stable community, one that serves in relative independence from the local bishop. If the diocesan priest (the "secular clergy") fits more naturally in the first model, the religious order priest (the "regular clergy") opens out into the second model.

Diversity in Communion

O'Malley's argument represents a particularly incisive articulation of a broader awareness that has been growing among religious order priests since the Vatican II. For the *ressourcement* promoted by the council was multifaceted. Alongside *Presbyterorum Ordinis*'s recovery of the patristic ideal of church order, there is *Perfectae Caritatis*'s call to religious congregations to return to the founding vision of

5. Ibid., 257.

their orders, the original inspiration and distinctive charisms of their particular communities.

Despite the tendency of postconciliar teaching to lump all religious communities together under the rubric of the evangelical counsels—the common commitment to vows of poverty, chastity, and obedience—when we look at the histories, the spiritualities, and above all the ministries that have marked these various communities, what we see is incredible diversity. This is so much the case that the title of one of O'Malley's essays on the subject, "One Priesthood: Two Traditions," seems a vast understatement.[6] Within the one tradition of religious order priests, there are in fact many, many traditions.

This awareness of diversity has not had the kind of impact you would expect on the broader theological conversation about church and ministry. Despite all the great historical work, systematic ecclesiology still seems enamored of the patristic ideal. Nowhere is this more clear than in the prominence given to an ecclesiology of communion in recent decades. This thoroughly patristic paradigm of church—trinitarian, eucharistic, bishop-centric—took off in the 1980s, in part as the magisterium's response to the perceived ecclesiological confusion of the postconciliar period. The 1985 Extraordinary Synod of Bishops reread Vatican II through the lens of *communio*, concluding, "For the Church, there is only one way into the future: the way pointed by the Council, the full implementation of the Council and its communion ecclesiology."[7] Before becoming Pope Benedict XVI, Joseph Ratzinger spoke of communion ecclesiology as the "one basic ecclesiology."[8]

Communion ecclesiology has also become an important framework for ecumenical dialogue. It appears in numerous bilateral and multilateral ecumenical reports, including the following milestones: (1) the 1993 World Conference on Faith and Order, which took as its theme *Towards Koinonia in Faith, Life and Witness*; (2) the 2004 text of the US Lutheran-Catholic Dialogue, *The Church as Koinonia*

6. O'Malley, "One Priesthood: Two Traditions," 9.

7. Extraordinary Synod of Bishops, "The Final Report," in *Origins* 15 (19 December 1985): 444–50, at 448.

8. Joseph Ratzinger, "Ultimately There Is One Basic Ecclesiology," *L'Osservatore Romano*, English ed., 17 June 1992, 1.

of Salvation: Its Structures and Ministries; and (3) the 2013 study document put out by the World Council of Churches' Faith and Order Commission, *The Church: Towards a Common Vision.*[9]

There are good reasons why communion has caught on in ecumenical circles. The term *koinonia* appears throughout the New Testament and in the writings of the early church. It evokes a shared history of church order that predates our ecclesial divisions. Within Catholic ecclesiology, the approach has been fruitful. In the work of theologians like Walter Kasper, Jean-Marie Tillard, Hervé-Marie Legrand, Joseph Komonchak, Susan Wood, and Richard Gaillardetz, this patristic vision of communion opens out into creative ways of talking about ministerial relationships in the present.[10]

So I do not want to dismiss this model out of hand. And yet, I do want to insist that communion ecclesiology does not capture the full ministerial diversity of our past, nor should it constrain the ministerial opportunities of our present.

It may be that we have already turned a corner. The various efforts of Pope Francis to shift our focus from maintenance to mission mark the most dramatic conversion in this regard. Not only in his call to the peripheries, his care for the marginalized, his challenge to structures of exclusion, and his constant talk of becoming missionary disciples, but also in his deepest philosophical and theological commitments, Pope Francis invites us into a paradigm shift. Time is greater than space. The whole is greater than the part. Unity before conflict. Realities are more important than ideas.[11]

---

9. See World Conference on Faith and Order, *Towards Koinonia in Faith, Life and Witness: Message, Section Reports, Discussion Paper* (Geneva: WCC Publications, 1993); Randall Lee and Jeffrey Gros, eds., *The Church as Koinonia of Salvation: Its Structures and Ministries* (Washington, DC: USCCB Publishing, 2004); Faith and Order Commission, *The Church: Towards a Common Vision*, Faith and Order Paper No. 214 (Geneva: WCC Publications, 2013).

10. See Edward P. Hahnenberg, "The Mystical Body of Christ and Communion Ecclesiology: Historical Parallels," *Irish Theological Quarterly* 70 (2005): 3–30; Dennis M. Doyle, *Communion Ecclesiology: Visions and Versions* (Maryknoll, NY: Orbis, 2000).

11. See Francis, *Evangelii Gaudium* (The Joy of the Gospel), apostolic exhortation (Vatican City: Libreria Editrice Vaticana, 2013), 222–37, http://w2.vatican.va/content/francesco/en/apost_exhortations/documents/papa-francesco_esortazione-ap_20131124_evangelii-gaudium.html. On Francis's philosophical

Blueprint Ecclesiologies or the Concrete Church

What does all of this mean for the ecclesiologist? What does it mean for the theologian of ministry? In simplest terms, it means: Do not teach from above; instead learn from below. What I intend to highlight here is a kind of methodological reorientation that, among other things, keeps theologians like me from coming in and telling religious order priests what priesthood in religious life is all about. To do that would be to make ideas more important than realities—which is a constant temptation for academics, particularly academics of a more systematic bent. The temptation lurking in my argument so far is to conclude with something like this: As religious priests, you should not understand your experience as "patristic and pastoral," you should understand your experience as "modern and missionary." But to do so would simply replace one idealistic European model with another idealistic European model. Instead, the discipline for the theologian is to begin by asking: *What is your experience?*

Several years ago, theologian Nicholas Healy complained about "blueprint ecclesiologies." By this term he meant the tendency of so much of modern ecclesiology to reflect on the church abstractly from above—to set up an ideal vision, a blueprint, "a more or less complete description of what the perfect church should look like," and to judge ecclesial realities like ministry in light of that ideal.[12] Healy challenged ecclesiologists, instead of focusing on ideal types, to make the proper subject of their study the "concrete church," which is not to be understood as the visible church, opposed to the spiritual church. Rather, it is to be understood as the theological reality of the church (which is infused with God's Spirit)—the reality of the church's agency in history, its human, social, limited existence and activity in time.

Since then, there has been growing interest among Catholic ecclesiologists in the "concrete church," if not in Healy's particular alter-

---

background, see Thomas R. Rourke, *The Roots of Pope Francis's Social and Political Thought: From Argentina to the Vatican* (Lanham, MD: Rowman & Littlefield, 2016).

12. Nicholas M. Healy, *Church, World and the Christian Life: Practical-Prophetic Ecclesiology* (Cambridge: Cambridge University Press, 2000), 36.

native proposal. We see it in different ways: in the excellent sociological studies of priesthood by scholars such as Sr. Katarina Schuth, Dean Hoge, and others;[13] in the three-volume work of Roger Haight, *Christian Community in History;*[14] in the conversations surrounding "comparative ecclesiology" and "ecclesiology from below" that were sparked by that project;[15] in attempts to engage the social sciences;[16] in the Ecclesiology and Ethnography Network coming out of the United Kingdom;[17] in Catholic contributions to the field of "lived religion."[18] More and more we are asking: What is happening in the church? What is happening in ministry? But the question remains: What does this mean for a theology of church? What does this mean for a theology of ministry?

Implications for a Theology of Ministry

Earlier I stressed O'Malley's point that most postconciliar Catholic theologies of ministry are marred by a fifteen-hundred-year-long blind spot—a tendency to skip quickly from the biblical and patristic periods right to Vatican II, dismissing everything in between as dark,

13. See Katarina Schuth, *Priestly Ministry in Multiple Parishes* (Collegeville, MN: Liturgical Press, 2006); Dean R. Hoge and Jacqueline E. Wenger, *Evolving Visions of the Priesthood: Changes from Vatican II to the Turn of the New Century* (Collegeville, MN: Liturgical Press, 2003); Hoge and Wenger, *Seminary Formation: Recent History, Current Circumstances, New Directions* (Collegeville, MN: Liturgical Press, 2016); Charles E. Zech et al., *Catholic Parishes of the 21st Century* (New York: Oxford University Press, 2017).

14. Roger Haight, *Christian Community in History*, 3 vols. (New York: Continuum, 2004, 2005, 2008).

15. See Gerard Mannion, ed., *Comparative Ecclesiology: Critical Investigations* (London: T & T Clark, 2008).

16. See Neil Ormerod, *Re-Visioning the Church: An Experiment in Systematic-Historical Ecclesiology* (Minneapolis: Fortress Press, 2014).

17. See Pete Ward, ed., *Perspectives on Ecclesiology and Ethnography* (Grand Rapids, MI: William B. Eerdmans, 2012); Christian B. Scharen, ed., *Explorations in Ecclesiology and Ethnography* (Grand Rapids, MI: William B. Eerdmans, 2012).

18. See Claire E. Wolfteich and Annemie Dillen, *Catholic Approaches in Practical Theology: International and Interdisciplinary Perspectives* (Leuven: Peeters, 2016).

dysfunctional, "medieval," and irrelevant to church life in the modern world. I only briefly mentioned the reasons O'Malley sees behind this historical bias. One seems particularly germane here: the tendency to rely too heavily on official documents and thus focus on ideas about ministry, instead of examining what was actually happening "on the ground" through the study of unofficial sources such as letters, diaries, and reports from the field.

Take O'Malley's favorite example, the sixteenth century. As I said, during this period, Catholic ministry went through one of its most innovative and exciting transformations in history. But reading the decrees of the Council of Trent, you would never know it. The mendicant orders saw tremendous growth in both size and influence; and new apostolic orders like the Jesuits burst onto the scene, experimenting with everything from directing retreats, spiritual counseling, and social ministries to using schools, artists, and the press as instruments of ministry. The catechesis, evangelization, and missionary outreach was intense, immense, and unprecedented—a thrust seen nowhere more dramatically than in the massive efforts directed toward evangelizing the newly "discovered" worlds of the Americas and Asia. But, as O'Malley observes, just as this global missionary movement was at its peak in the mid-sixteenth century, the bishops gathered at Trent bypassed it "without a word."[19]

Over the past fifty years, we have grown accustomed to citing the documents of Vatican II in order to explain the new vision of church, ministry, and priesthood that has taken root in our Catholic communities. But is that adequate? Does the council exhaust our understanding of the conciliar period? I do not mean to dismiss the documents. But try to imagine some future scholar, five hundred years from now, looking back in time, and attempting to describe priesthood in religious life during the Vatican II era simply by citing *Presbyterorum Ordinis* or *Perfectae Caritatis*. Are our theologies already guilty of starting with ideas about church, ideas about ministry, priesthood, or religious life, instead of looking to what the Spirit might be revealing though the concrete experience of this postconciliar period?

Another church historian, Massimo Faggioli, expands on the point about the Council of Trent by linking it explicitly to Vatican II. He

19. O'Malley, "One Priesthood: Two Traditions," 17.

stresses the importance of reflecting on realities and not just on words. So much of what today can be legitimately considered "Tridentine," Faggioli argues, cannot be found in the published decrees of the Council of Trent. The distinctive elements of the Tridentine church—its new ministries and religious orders, its institutional and juridical structures, its centralized and universalist ecclesiology, its liturgy, rites, and catechism—owe more to the reception of the council than to the corpus of its documents. If our assessment of Trent is not limited to commenting on its texts, Faggioli asks, why should we feel so constrained when it comes to Vatican II? Drawing a line from the sixteenth century to the present, he concludes that "refuting the theological value of the reception of Vatican II" is freezing Vatican II "in a sort of theological monolith—assigning it a fate that had not even been the one of the Council of Trent."[20]

I suggest taking this observation one step further. It is important to hold the documents of Vatican II within the context of the total event of Vatican II—the whole movement of *ressourcement* leading up to it, the *aggiornamento* flowing out of it—because holding it all together allows us to understand the council not only historically, but also theologically. In other words, the reception of Vatican II is theologically significant. The reception of Vatican II, arguably, will have greater lasting impact on the church than its documents. The experience of priesthood in religious life these past fifty years—as one example of this reception—is likewise theologically significant. From some future vantage point, I believe, the experience of religious order priests will prove just as influential on the theological tradition and the development of doctrine as *Presbyterorum Ordinis* and *Perfectae Caritatis*.

Conclusion

The reception of Vatican II is a global phenomenon. Karl Rahner famously described the council as Catholicism's first step toward a

20. Massimo Faggioli, *A Council for the Global Church: Receiving Vatican II in History* (Minneapolis: Fortress Press, 2015), 256.

"world church."[21] It is good to underscore the words "first step." The level of international participation at Vatican II was no doubt unprecedented in the history of councils; however, the major players, the major issues, and the major audiences were still by and large European. Much of what we have seen in the church around the world since the council was unforeseen by those who participated in it.

The "reception" of Vatican II was not simply an "implementation" of its decrees. Instead of implementing the council, what local churches did was to "welcome" it. The process of reception was not a one-directional act of transmission or teaching; rather, it was a reciprocal encounter. Local churches "welcomed" the council. When we welcome a guest into our home, the dynamic of our family and the rhythm of the household adapt. We are changed by the presence of another. At the same time—particularly if the stay is extended—the family dynamic and household rhythm have an effect on the visitor. The guest is changed, even transformed, by time in our home. In a similar way, in welcoming Vatican II, local churches are transformed by its teaching and at the same time transform its teaching in theologically significant ways.

How have religious communities that include ordained priests welcomed Vatican II into their homes? That question, I think, will have many answers. What is exciting about the reflections that follow is the glimpse they can give us into this experience of welcoming the council. These essays represent the reflections of members of religious communities from around the world; thus, they offer unique access to the global reception of Vatican II. From these experiences, I believe, will arise those insights into priesthood and religious life that will point out new ways forward.

21. See Karl Rahner, "Basic Theological Interpretation of the Second Vatican Council," and "The Abiding Significance of the Second Vatican Council," *Theological Investigations* 20 (New York: Crossroad, 1981), 77–89, 90–102.

Chapter 6

In Solidum: An Option for Religious?

David Szatkowski, SCJ

Parishes exist to make the church and the pastoral ministry of the church present in the world.[1] Naturally, this requires some regulation of the practical matters of running the parish. The Code of Canon Law regulates how parish ministry is to be structured. The structural model most familiar to us is the "one pastor in one parish" model. Parochial vicars are usually assigned to larger parishes where more priests are needed or due to some other particular need (ethnic minority, language, rite, etc.) in accord with canon 545. These vicars are appointed to help the pastor, to act with common counsel and effort in his ministry and to offer common counsel and collaborate in his ministry. "Vicar" in canon law means that you are exercising the power of another.[2]

This model of parochial ministry is the default model of the law.[3] There is nothing wrong with it. Religious priests have operated out of this structure and have given very effective pastoral ministry. But the law does provide another structure "when circumstances require it."[4] The alternative structure is a team of priests acting *in solidum*. I want to raise the question: Could the *in solidum* model give practical and legal assistance to how religious minister?

---

1. *Sacrosanctum Concilium* 42.
2. C. 131 §1–2.
3. See c. 515 §1.
4. C. 517 §1.

The inspiration for this reflection came from the council of formators at Catholic Theological Union. A member of that council said that his community requires at least three religious ministers in a parish. If the staffing requirement is not possible—if, for example, the parish is a "one-man" parish—his community is not able to give pastoral care to that parish, since the ministry situation would create a living situation contrary to their religious life. The problem is that diocesan ministry structures do not always meet the needs of religious communities' lifestyles. Tension can arise between the balance of community life and ministry, between how we as religious live a charism and the parochial structure within which we may minister. I believe that in some cases the *in solidum* structure of parochial ministry allows for a better expression of a religious charism in ministry.

I hope to help others consider whether or not the *in solidum* model may be a good legal structure for their parochial ministry. To do this I will give consideration to the concept of "parish." I hope that through understanding the concept of the parish, we can consider parish ministry more broadly.

The Concept of "Parish"

The current legal definition of a parish is found in canon 515 §1–3:

> A parish is a certain community of the Christian faithful stably constituted in a particular church, whose pastoral care is entrusted to a pastor (*parochus*[5]) as its proper pastor (*pastor*) under the authority of the diocesan bishop.
>
> It is only for the diocesan bishop to erect, suppress, or alter parishes. He is neither to erect, suppress, nor alter parishes, unless he has heard the presbyteral council.
>
> A legitimately erected parish possesses juridic personality by the law itself.

---

5. *Parochus*: "parish priest, pastor, benefice." Leo Stelten, *Dictionary of Ecclesiastical Latin* (Peabody, MA: Hendrickson, 1995), 186. All Latin translations are from this work.

A parish is a "certain community." A diocese is "a portion of the people of God."[6] A parish *is not* a particular church;[7] a parish is *part of* a particular church. Parishes cannot ever be separated from the diocese any more than a diocese can be separated from the universal church. Parishes are normally territorial, but can be a "certain community" of rite, language, or nationality, or based around "some other reason."[8] Pope St. John Paul II reminded us that no parish is an abstract reality. Therefore, no single situation meets every need.

Parishes exist to give pastoral care to all the people of the parish.[9] Certainly there is sacramental care, but pastoral care encompasses much more. Pastoral care includes discussion of how the church can help address real-world problems, catechesis, social outreach, liturgical worship, spiritual direction, and all the other ministries that we see. Pastoral care is anything that makes the presence of Christ felt in the community of both the faithful and the nonfaithful.[10] The fundamental difference between a parish engaging in these works and another institution doing the same thing is that the parish does ministry in the name of Christ, who is acting through the faithful of the parish.

Religious Life—Unique Life and Legal Demands

My focus is *religious* priesthood. For that reason, I wish to name some juridic requirements of religious life. I will not consider religious life in its totality or any particular proper law; my goal is to name certain universal juridic concepts about religious institutes that are relevant. Religious life has two specific characteristics: public

---

6. C. 369.

7. See Francisco Ramos, *Le Chiese particolari e i loro raggruppamenti* (Roma: @ Millennium 2000, 2000), 512.

8. C. 518.

9. See Antonio Sánchez-Gil, "Commentary on canon 515," in *Exegetical Commentary on the Code of Canon Law*, vol. II/2, ed. Ángel Marzoa, Jorge Miras, and Rafael Rodriguez-Ocana, English gen. ed. Ernest Caparros (Montreal: Wilson & Lafleur/Chicago, IL: Midwest Theological Forum, 2004), 1256. Hereafter, *Exegetical Commentary* for all works from this series.

10. See c. 528 §1 for an example.

vows and common life.[11] Proper law regulates how the vows and common life are to be observed.

Since all religious are obligated to live in a house (*domus*) of the institute,[12] it should come as no surprise that religious have a right to live according to the proper purpose and spirit of the institute.[13] When the bishop gives consent to erect a house in his diocese, he gives *ipso iure* the right to live according to the spirit and purpose of the institute.[14] If a religious community has a particular law of *how* to live religious life (number of members, balance of community and apostolate, etc.), that right is maintained when a house is erected.

Having the care of a parish does not dispense a religious from common life. We would never say that being a pastor dispenses a religious from the observation of the vow of poverty, so why would we say it dispenses him from common life? While ministry can be a legitimate reason not to live in a house of the institute,[15] if another option is available, I would suggest that the weight of the law's preference is to the observation of common life. This protects the eschatological value of the common life.[16]

There are times when a diocesan bishop will want religious working in his diocese to live alone if the parish is a "one-man" parish. This reflects the value of the pastor living in a rectory near the church as a diocesan priest would.[17] Both religious life and diocesan priesthood are invaluable gifts to the church, but they are two distinct and different vocations. Each deserves to be recognized for itself and as bringing something different to the church. Religious are not diocesan priests and should not imitate their way of life if that can be avoided. In fact the law calls for the bishop to help the community to preserve

11. See c. 607 §2.
12. See c. 665 §1.
13. See c. 610 §1.
14. See cc. 609 §1; 611 §1°.
15. See c. 665 §1.
16. See John Paul II, *Vita Consecrata* (VC), post-synodal apostolic exhortation (Vatican City: Libreria Editrice Vatican, 1996), 42.
17. See c. 533 §1.

its way of living, not seek exceptions to it, even in cases where religious are ministers in the diocese.[18]

The present Code emphasizes this reality in canon 678 §1–2:

> Religious are subject to the power of bishops whom they are bound to follow with devoted submission and reverence in those matters which regard the care of souls, the public exercise of divine worship, and other works of the apostolate.
>
> In exercising an external apostolate, religious are also subject to their proper superiors and must remain faithful to the discipline of the institute. The bishops themselves are not to fail to urge this obligation if the case warrants it.

There is no intent to create opposition between bishops and religious. Each has a proper sphere and gives authentic service to the church. But there are distinctions: with regard to public ministry, the bishop is to be given submission and reverence. But this reverence should not come at the expense of the discipline of the institute. John Paul II taught that common life may be *adapted* (see VC 37). The reason to adapt the common life is for fidelity to the *mission*. The *mission* calls for the adapting of forms, but always in light of the inspiration of the founder. Religious are not "slot fillers" to a diocesan ministry. Ministry must be evaluated in light of the institute's charism and way of living. The community must examine particular parishes to see if they truly fit the charismatic life of the community. The questions "Will this charism benefit this parish?" and "Can we and how will we live our charism in ministry to this parish?" must always be asked in the mutual discernment of the religious superiors and diocesan bishop.

In Solidum

I will now focus on the model *in solidum*. The *in solidum* model was not created for the good of religious, but the law does offer it. For this reason, I believe individual communities should be willing to

---

18. See c. 678 §2.

evaluate this model to see if it is an effective way for them to minister.

Even when religious accept a parish, the model of a single pastor and parish can still be exercised, and parochial vicars can be part of that parish ministry.[19] It could be for any number of good reasons the best model available. But it is not the only model the law allows.

Canon 517 §1 states:

> When circumstances require it [*ubi adiuncta id requirant*], the pastoral care of a parish or different parishes together can be entrusted to several priests *in solidum*, with the requirement, however, that in exercising pastoral care one of them must be the moderator, namely, the one who is to direct the joint action and to answer for it to the bishop.

The model may be used "when circumstances require it." The verb *requirere* is used.[20] This is a more restrictive verb than *suadere*[21] or *opportunuum censere*.[22] This restrictive nature was intended.[23] *Suadere* is used in other places when the Code intends "convenience."[24]

Antonio Sánchez-Gil argues that the canon is restrictive and that the *in solidum* model is to be used only when there is a certain need and the more traditional models are "considerably difficult" to use.[25] Among the situations that Sánchez-Gil foresees as "required" are: dioceses that have few priests, who also have other jobs in one or more parishes, and therefore one would assume also hold offices in

19. See c. 545 §1–2.

20. *Requirere*: "need, require, seek, ask after, demand, search for." Stelten, *Dictionary of Ecclesiastical Latin*, 230.

21. *Suadere*: "persuade, exhort, advise, urge, suggest, recommend, propose"; *censere*: "think, approve, estimate, call." Ibid., 255.

22. See Ramos, *Le Chiese particolari*, 544. See also Jorge Miras, "El ejercicio 'in solidum' del ministerio parroquiale," in *Ius Canonicum* 29 (1989); 483–502.

23. See Pontificia Commissio Codici Iuris Canonici Recognoscendo, "Liber II De populo Dei (cann. 201–502)," *Communicationes* 14 (1982): 221.

24. Antonio Sánchez-Gil, "Commentary on canon 515," in *Exegetical Commentary*, vol. II/2, 1268; cf. Miras, "El ejecicio 'in solidum,'" 495.

25. Sánchez-Gil, "Commentary on canon 515," in *Exegetical Commentary*, vol. II/2, 1268.

the diocesan curia in addition to parochial responsibilities; overpopulated parishes in large dioceses; scattered and small rural parishes, so that each parish has a direct relationship with each priest; promotion of coresponsibility in pastoral ministry and communal life among priests.[26] Sánchez-Gil is not alone in seeing this canon as having very restricted use. Jorge Miras and Cardinal Francesco Coccopalmerio agree that *in solidum* cannot be used when the more traditional model is available.[27]

Rights and Duties of the Priest Team *in solidum*

Let us begin by looking at what canon 543 §1–2 states:

> If the pastoral care of some parish or of different parishes together is entrusted to priests *in solidum*, each of them is obliged to perform the tasks and functions of pastor mentioned in cann. 528, 529, and 530 according to the arrangement they establish. All of them have the faculty of assisting at marriages and all the powers to dispense granted to a pastor by law; these are to be exercised, however, under the direction of the moderator.
>
> All the priests who belong to the group:
> 1° are bound by the obligation of residence;
> 2° are to establish through common counsel an arrangement by which one of them is to celebrate a Mass for the people according to the norm of can. 534;
> 3° the moderator alone represents in juridic affairs of the parish or parishes entrusted to the group.

Canon 543 says that "pastoral care" is entrusted to the "priests *in solidum*" and refers to the canons that describe the ministry of a pastor. Those canons demonstrate that the pastor (here, all the priests) is to have a personal and pastoral relationship to the people served. Therefore, with a team of priests *in solidum*, each priest truly has the same pastoral, spiritual, and legal relationship with the people he serves and does not exercise the pastoral authority of another.

26. See ibid.
27. See Miras, "El ejercicio 'in solidum,'" 496.

Put another way, this is one office with multiple holders of that office.[28] The *Exegetical Commentary* explains the relationship of the priests in this way:[29]

> The juridical nature of the parochial ministry entrusted *in solidum* consists precisely in that the pastoral care of one or several parishes [is given to a priest team]. This may be considered as a single pastoral task, and is entrusted to several priests at the same time so that they co-responsibly exercise their function by joint effort. Consequently, each priest receives *identical participation* in the entrusted office and can perform the functions that are attributed to a parish priest (can. 543,1). . . . As the codifying Commission [for the Revision of the Code] stated, the moderator, who is *primus inter pares*, directs the joint action and is responsible for it to the bishop.

I want to talk first about what is meant by "team" and then return to the moderator. Because of the nature of this ministry, all members of the team must all meet the requirements of canon 521 (be a priest; be outstanding in doctrine, morals, and zeal for souls; possess the qualities of universal or particular law necessary to care for the parish in question; and be clearly suitable to the office), and they must be installed in office.[30]

"Team" here means that all of the priests are equally capable of performing the tasks of canons 528–30, tasks normally entrusted to the pastor. The canon allows the priests on the team to decide *how* they will make these things happen. This is truly a decision that the team makes as a team. The team could therefore decide on common policies about baptism, marriage preparation, assistance with visiting the infirm, etc. In addition, the priests among themselves decide who will celebrate the *missa pro populo* (and where it will be celebrated, if there is more than one parish).[31]

28. See Miras, "El ejercicio 'in solidum,'" 497.

29. Sánchez-Gil, "Commentary on canon 517," in *Exegetical Commentary*, vol. II/2, 1267–68.

30. See c. 542 §1–3.

31. See cc. 534, 543 §2, 2°.

The team is not a college, nor are team members a council to the moderator, as canon 127 would define these things. For example, in religious life, we think of a provincial and his council. In those cases, we all know that some acts (such as religious profession) require a vote.[32] "Team" in this context means that all the priests are equal. In these pastoral matters, they come to decision about how to proceed. Each priest has the pastoral care of the people of God of that parish or parishes, even though he does not receive the title of "parish priest." He does not share in the ministry of another, for each is equally the minister.[33] Each member of the team enjoys all the pastoral power enumerated above.[34] The team must decide on how to use the gifts of each individual most effectively so that the best possible care is provided. It is for the team to decide the best method for accomplishing the pastoral work assigned to it.

The Figure of the Moderator of the Team *in solidum*

The figure of the moderator is required. And there can only be one moderator.[35] The moderator, I suggest, should be named in the same decree of the bishop that appoints the team. I would further suggest that this follow the same appointment protocol as for a pastor, which for religious is usually by presentation.[36] The canon, 158 §1, states that ecclesiastical office can be filled by presentation. Often, a religious superior presents a particular cleric for the office of pastor and the bishop then appoints him. Canon 543 does not speak of the team having the right to present a moderator, but common sense suggests that they should all at least find the moderator acceptable or individual members could refuse to be appointed in accordance with canon 159.

---

32. See c. 656 §3.

33. See Luigi Sabbarese, *La costituzione gerarchica della Chiesa universale e particolare. Commento al Coddice di Diritto Canonic Libero II, Parte II*, 2nd ed. (Vatican City: Urbaniana University Press, 2001), 206.

34. See Ramos, *Le Chiese particolari*, 547.

35. See c. 526 §2.

36. See cc. 158–163 for the laws of presentation.

The moderator is the *primus inter pares*[37] and not an executive chairman or the "über-pastor." The moderator is not separate or over the team, but an organic part of it. Neither is the moderator a religious superior. The ministry is equal among all the priests. Yet the moderator is to "direct" the ministry and answer for the team to the bishop according to canon 517. Canon 543 §1 tells us that marriages and dispensations are to be done under the direction of the moderator.

So what is "under direction," and how does the moderator "direct the ministry" of the team? There is a variety of opinions among commentators on this subject. It is possible that the bishop could give specific authority to one or another in the group in some particular matter. It is possible that the group could submit a specific way of functioning (sort of a by-laws) to the bishop that, once he approves, the team always uses.[38]

I would suggest that the moderator—as the first among equals—be responsible to ensure that the team meets all of its responsibilities. In part, this is a work of coordination. How the group arrives at distributing the ministry is part of the responsibility of the whole team. Once the team makes a decision, the moderator continues to hold the team accountable to itself and to the bishop. The moderator is responsible to report to the bishop what is being done and how it is being done.

I believe the moderator has the right to ensure that everything is done according to the law (either proper or universal). Examples could be: that premarital preparation be done according to the norms of the diocese, that the baptismal register be maintained and sacraments recorded,[39] that the various programs for the protection of God's children take place, and similar kinds of things. When the bishop comes for visitation,[40] the moderator meets with the bishop and informs him about the team's ministry and submits any expected reports.

---

37. Antonio Sanchez-Gil, "Commentary on canon 517," in *Exegetical Commentary*, vol. II/2, 1267.

38. Ibid., 1371–2.

39. See c. 535 §2.

40. See c. 396 §1.

The canon states that all priests have the faculty to assist at marriage and give dispensations that the pastor can give, but that these are to be done under the direction of the moderator. Clearly this is not about an ability to act; each priest can act. The question is how the team is to act. The moderator does not give "permission" for a priest to act, but rather he ensures that all pastoral care is done with uniformity and justice. In the case of marriage, the team must ensure that no one priest is overly burdened with marriages and marriage preparation.

Canon 543 §2, 3° gives the moderator alone the right to represent the *juridic affairs* of the parish or parishes entrusted to the group. Canon 532, which is part of the ministry of the pastor, refers to canons 1281–88. These canons regulate the administration of the temporal goods. So here we would name things like budgets, the hiring and firing of employees, entering into contracts, selling or buying property, and other similar acts. I would also add that matters dealing with pastoral councils and finance councils in the parishes should be reserved to the moderator.

Considerations for a Team

The canons, not surprisingly, do not specify what a member of the team has to be or do beyond the requirements of canon 521, which means that each member of the team must have the same qualifications as a pastor. But beyond this, what else should be considered? I would suggest that there are some practical matters.

First, the major superior must realize that the team is going to be appointed *in solidum*, not as individuals. The appointment follows the norms of a pastor.[41] This means particular people will be holding office for a fixed (or indefinite) period of time. This team is appointed together, so members cannot be changed without observing the formalities of an appointment. While canon 682 does allow a religious to be recalled by a superior, this team should have reasonable stability. The major superior must ask: Can I invest this number of people in this ministry for a reasonable length of time?

41. See cc. 522, 524.

Second, there must be some pastoral maturity in the members of the team. In the team, there is no parochial vicar as foreseen by canon 545. If you have a newly ordained priest, he may need mentorship. He may not yet have the pastoral experience to function in this way. Another situation would be a priest who has some specific limitation; he may be a wonderful assistant or be capable of limited ministry, but could not function without greater supervision.

Third, the team must be able to work together. Earlier, I said that religious priests are not slot fillers. The same is true of a team. The major superior must ask the proposed religious: Would you want to be a part of this kind of ministry? Not everyone will do well with this structure. Are the members of the proposed team willing to commit to this common approach?

Fourth, are there circumstances requiring this model? Earlier, I did say that geography, size of the parishes, and priests living together are all reasons to consider this model. Naturally, this is not an exhaustive list. But they are considerations.

For religious, who are called to live together, the obligation of residence in the parish could result in a religious living apart from other pastoral ministers if there are multiple rectories. Canon 543 §2 1° gives the *team* the obligation of residence in the territory being served (in the one or more parishes). Sometimes religious work in relatively rural areas. For example, my community serves six parishes in four counties in northern Mississippi. The religious work as a team *in solidum* in those parishes and share a common residence. Incidentally, the fact that the religious all share the pastoral responsibility also allows the salaries to be shared among the parishes. There are three salaries, not six.

Fifth, will the bishop agree to this model? This consideration is an absolute requirement. It is the bishop who is going to make these appointments. This model is one concrete way in which religious and bishops could work together to meet particular pastoral needs of the diocese and the way of living of a particular religious institute.

Sixth, I believe the collaboration has intrinsic witness value for the parish and the church. Part of the gift of religious life and ministry is showing forth a prophetic way of living and ministering. If a community is allowed to minister together, I believe the charism of a particular community is made more evident. In considering a team *in solidum*, I do believe it a reasonable question to ask: Will this model allow our charism to be experienced? Will this model allow us to minister out of the spirit of the institute? The common goal of both the bishop and the religious involved is pastoral care in a structure that promotes good order and good ministry. Could the parish's experience of the institute's charism be taken into consideration when choosing a method of pastoral ministry?

What *In Solidum* Is Not

The team is a means of delivering pastoral care. The parish or parishes being served are not being merged or altered. So if a religious community is using *in solidum* to serve three parishes, the financial affairs of all three parishes remain distinct and separate. The property, goods, and juridic affairs remain separate, despite cooperation that may exist.

In this model, the bishop is not entrusting a parish to someone not a priest. The reasonable question may arise: Can a member of my institute who is not a priest be on this team as a pastoral minister? I would answer that *in sensu stricto*, the answer is no. Canon 543 *does not* foresee laypeople (whether or not they are religious) as being members of the *in solidum* team. However, another religious (either of the team's own institute or that of another) could certainly be part of the parish staff.

The question may also arise: Could the ministry *in solidum* be done as a collaboration between religious of different communities or between religious and diocesan priests? The answer would be yes, but the major superiors and bishops in question would have to agree in advance. In addition, the proposed team would have to resolve how *they* would function as a team.

Conclusion

My hope is that this chapter encourages members of religious institutes to think differently about parish ministry. The brief historical consideration reminds the reader that the church's structures to give pastoral care have evolved over time and will continue to evolve to meet the needs of the people of God. I hope that my raising up of some of Vatican II's teaching encourages readers to think broadly and creatively about the role of the parish in modern society.

I hope that my sharing the *in solidum* model helps readers to see a different way to approach parish ministry. As readers continue to consider how best to serve God's people in their own context, I hope I have encouraged them to ask the question, "Could this fit our reality?"

Chapter 7

Becoming a Cross-Cultural Person

Anthony J. Gittins, CSSp

Introduction

There is a significant point of clarification to be made before we proceed: the title for this workshop was "Crossing Cultures." But since a culture is not an entity like a bridge or a river, no one can "cross" a culture; rather one enters into it as one might enter the ocean or an unfamiliar environment. We must be careful not to concretize or reify what is both a concept and a process or way of being experienced by a social group. Given that each of us is a member of a particular culture—with its characteristic traditions, beliefs, behaviors, and available alternatives and choices—we can easily visualize two contrasting cultures and identify them as cultures A and B. Should a person of culture A succeed in leaving that cultural environment and becoming immersed in culture B, we can call such a person "cross-cultural." The issue of whether, by whom, and how this might be undertaken constitutes our topic.

The specific context of our reflections is religious life and priesthood, but my starting point is the universal call to discipleship; religious and clergy are simply particular expressions of myriad responses to this call. Every baptized person is called to discipleship, which Pope Francis explicitly identifies as "missionary discipleship."[1] Since

---

1. Francis, *Evangelii Gaudium* (EG [The Joy of the Gospel]), apostolic exhortation (Vatican City: Libreria Editrice Vaticana, 2013), 27, 40, 119–20.

there is no such thing as generic discipleship, each person must learn from Jesus and discover how to live discipleship in his or her particular circumstances. But one element of discipleship that applies to everyone is that it should be expressed in terms of boundary crossing and centrifugal movement: it cannot be legitimately incarnated simply by living within a comfortable, familiar, and controlled world. Discipleship calls us to conversion—to God, to "the other," and to "culture." But, given our initial *caveat*, culture is a word that refers to actual people in actual social contexts, as well as to their way of life, the traces they leave on the environment, and their understanding of life's meaning and purpose.

Discipleship for Contemporary Religious Clergy

When we explore the universal call to discipleship as it applies more specifically to the religious priesthood, we can note some of the aspects of Jesus' own ministry that we might identify as truly integral to his mission. Today there is a wide consensus that a cluster of four emblematic features can be described as integral to evangelization: each is intrinsic to the mission of Jesus, and no single one describes or covers it adequately. They are encounter, table fellowship, foot washing, and boundary crossing. Pope Francis identifies each of these, and we shall return to them in the final section, when considering an appropriate spirituality for cross-cultural living for clergy and religious.

When we apply these criteria to our own ministry as disciples of Jesus, it becomes obvious that they demand considerable movement on our part. And if we rise to the challenge, we will discover that we are called to become cross-cultural persons.

Cross-Culturality

Each of us is a person of culture, but none of us is born with culture. Enculturation, or socialization, is the process whereby a particular person becomes a person of a particular culture, through learning, discipline, experimentation, and experience. In principle, any baby could become a member of any culture. A baby born in Nigeria of

Igbo parents will, under normal circumstances, grow up to be culturally (as well as ethnically) Igbo. But the very same baby, transported to Chicago and adopted by Hispanic parents, will grow up to be culturally Hispanic-American (though ethnically of course, Igbo). Put simply, ethnicity is who we are; culture is how we live.

Let us call a person's own primary culture his or her "culture A" and identify the cultures of other people as B, C, D, and so on. If a person were to leave their culture A and "cross over," as it were, into a different culture, then, under certain conditions—but this is by no means automatic—that person could become a cross-cultural person. But simply leaving home does not make a person cross-cultural. So what are those conditions? On the part of the person aspiring to become cross-cultural, intentionality and commitment to learning the unfamiliar culture are required. And on the part of the host community, acceptance and legitimation of the outsider's status in his or her new environment are essential. Critically, only the insider community can confer legitimacy on the outsider, the stranger. But there are two kinds of outsiders—"nonparticipating" and "participating"—and a stranger only becomes an authentic cross-cultural person by being accepted as a "participating outsider" in the insiders' social world. The cross-cultural person will never become an insider and is always to some degree displaced or "out of place," while everyone else is "at home."

If would-be cross-cultural persons graciously accept their outsider status, show a real and continuous willingness to learn from and about the host community, and are able—over time—to convince the hosts that they truly wish to collaborate and contribute, then, precisely as outsider *participants* in the life and welfare of the insiders, they can become accepted into a relationship of true mutuality or mutual interdependence (which is not the same thing as social equality). That means that both outsiders and the insiders discover new purposes and ways of collaborating in the common human quest but from different perspectives.

Jesus is an excellent example of some (not all) of the critical features of the cross-cultural person. He chose to leave the security of his own cultural and social world in order to encounter others, with a view to understanding their experience and contributing to their well-being. Some people accepted him, while others did not.

But his mission was as an itinerant, a stranger,[2] a focus of sometimes contradictory responses. The prologue of John's Gospel puts it succinctly (and I paraphrase, to better make the point): He came to his own people, but some of them did not accept him. But to all who did receive him, he gave power to become children of God (see John 1:11–12).

Becoming Cross-Cultural: The Process

A person becomes fully cross-cultural by (1) leaving home and a familiar social world, (2) crossing over into a previously unknown or unfamiliar cultural and linguistic world, and (3) learning the culture and language under the scrutiny of the community he or she seeks to enter, until (4) that community is satisfied that the incomer is not a threat but actually an ally and a resource. In the process, the cross-cultural person discovers how to move from being a rank outsider to becoming a real participant (though an outsider participant).

Entering into an unfamiliar cultural milieu, hoping to remain indefinitely among and contribute to the well-being of those who live there, is not done lightly or painlessly. The sociological literature identifies three typical stages in the process: preliminary, liminal, and postliminal—where *liminal* (from the Latin *limen*) refers to a threshold, an in-betweenness, a transition, or a socially ambiguous state. It also has a temporal dimension: the state continues for a certain but unspecified time, leaving the individual vulnerable and constantly scrutinized by the host community. The process may be aborted before stage three, either because the host-community expels the incoming stranger, or because he or she finds the situation intolerable and chooses to leave.

The first stage is the preliminary (preliminal) phase. An incomer may initially be accorded the status of guest, since hospitality is a prime cultural value. But though such hospitality serves to temper the stranger's feeling of strangeness, such indulgence does not last long. Very soon, the guest will be expected either to move on else-

---

2. It is worth reflecting on Matthew 25:35 ("*I was* a stranger") and Luke 24:18 ("Are you the only *stranger* in Jerusalem?") (NRSV).

where or to contribute to the host community, specifically on its terms, since the host community has a preexisting agenda to which the incomer must accommodate himself or herself. The host community therefore, holds the initiative.

Now begins the liminal, or transitional, phase: the raw experience of being caught in a kind of limbo, a "betwixt-and between," that can last indefinitely. The only predictable thing, as far as the guest-now-becoming-a-true-stranger is concerned, is the very unpredictability of events and the inconsistency of the host community's behavior. After having been briefly indulged, the stranger now experiences a degree of abandonment; after having received every possible help, he or she now experiences a time of testing and the rather painful discovery of personal ignorance, dependency, and sometimes childish mood changes. During this time, the host community is testing the incomer, assessing whether the stranger is a potential asset, threat, or parasite. The stranger needs to develop or discover many basic skills, such as how, on the one hand, to ask for help and, on the other, to show some initiative. But the stranger does not know the conventional rules of behavior and is quite possibly ignorant of the language. Learning the language can be a systematic process; learning the culture is certainly no easier and is far less systematic. It is but a short distance from brief moments of euphoria at one's achievements to dejection and perhaps depression at one's ignorance and helplessness. Yet all this is critically important and intrinsic to the nature of the liminal period (the "novitiate," if you like), where there is mutual inspection and assessment. But the insiders are always "at home" and in control, while the stranger is clearly not at home and sometimes quite lost and bewildered.

Though the liminal phase may last months or even years, in time both the stranger and the host community come to know each other better. But the stranger is in no position to dictate to the hosts; and the hosts are under no obligation to accept the stranger into their lives.

The shift from the liminal to the postliminal phase—when the stranger is accepted and included—can occur with surprising speed. Going from thinking that one will never adjust, never understand, never relax, to a pervasive feeling of well-being and even of belonging may happen literally in a matter of days. It is something similar to the experience, after months of struggle, of suddenly dreaming one night of actually speaking one's target-language fluently—or more dramatically of one's mother speaking a language she could not possibly know. This represents the breakthrough moment. Likewise, when the liminal experience suddenly gives way to the postliminal, it comes as a shock and a very pleasant surprise.

Now the stranger and the host have achieved mutual recognition and acceptance of their differences. The stranger—to reiterate—will never be an insider, but a participating outsider who engages in the life of the insiders in a way they approve of. In fact, the agenda of the insiders can subsequently change significantly as they come to respect and value the perceptions, experience, wisdom, and worth of the outsider.

Passing Over—and Coming Back: A Life in Three "Lands"

Notre Dame theologian John Dunne said insightfully that the "passing over and coming back . . . is the [greatest religious] adventure of our time."[3] We can consider the cross-cultural process as one of "passing over"—with its connotations not only of transition but of dying. And further, we can imagine the course of a dedicated life as consisting of passing over from one's "homeland," into a "wonderland," and back to a "newfoundland." This may be a helpful image and a way of understanding the shifting dynamics of social interaction and pastoral commitment in the course of a lifetime. These three words represent "ideal types": helpful oversimplifications that need to be carefully contextualized and evaluated.

The *homeland* is where we were born and raised, learned our culture and established our bearings, struck our cultural roots and formed our cultural identity. It is our first, enduring world, and it provides the context in and from which we interpret, evaluate, and respond to persons and events. It also shapes our ethnocentricity, since we cannot look out on the world and others except from our own perspective and through our own eyes. But both within the

---

3. John S. Dunne, *The Way of All the Earth: Experiments in Truth and Religion* (Notre Dame, IN: Notre Dame Press, 1978), ix–x, 180.

homeland and later as we venture farther afield, our ethnocentricity will be challenged as we encounter other people, other worlds, and other perspectives or ethnocentric biases.

It is, of course, necessary to have sound roots in order to grow strong. Far from cutting those roots when one embarks on the journey to the wonderland, we need to understand that without such grounding or rooting, there can be no branching out, flourishing, or fruiting in subsequent personal and pastoral encounters.

The *wonderland* is the world(s) beyond our own familiar homeland, a world where people are different from us, speak differently, act differently, and have different histories and experiences—some of which, for good or ill, may have been shaped by their encounters with the world we identify and probably cherish as our own homeland. When we encounter such a world however, it may not be seen as a wonderland at all, but a land and people to fear or even despise. The challenge for every cross-cultural traveler is to identify personal bias, establish a positive rather than a negative approach, and seek and find the dignity of personal and cultural differences. Not everyone succeeds, however, as some people are unable to conquer their xenophobia, racism, or generalized negative evaluations of "the other," whoever he or she or they may be. To speak of the wonderland, therefore, is to encourage people to look for the good, the dignified, the virtue, and the grace in unfamiliar worlds, rather than to preempt the subsequent interactions by seeing only what they judge to be bad because unfamiliar, undignified because different from our ways, and sinful rather than touched by grace. It is also worthwhile to ponder the corollary: to learn of and acknowledge our own arrogance, ignorance, and sinfulness, and to undertake to rise to the challenge of living with "the other" in the awareness that there is good and bad, sin and grace, prejudice and tolerance to be found in every person and every culture.

The wonderland experience can be immensely valuable to anyone and everyone willing to learn, to think differently, and to strive for mutual tolerance and respect. It is, however, unremittingly demanding and does not come without struggle, commitment, and not infrequent contrition.

Time was when people set sail for distant (wonder) lands with a view to giving their lives for and among "the other." In the past half century and more, however, there has been a radical modification of this one-way traffic. People who left their homeland to live as outsider participants in the wonderland discovered increasingly that they could, and might be required to, return home, for a variety of reasons other than to sicken and die. There was apostolic work to be done in their later lives. Moreover, life expectancy had increased since 1900 by up to 65 percent in many countries, which indicated a much longer active life for many. But far from returning to the familiar *homeland* they had left years before, they now found themselves strangers in a strange land—their own—for this was not the *homeland* they had known and loved. Social change, globalization, and secularization had changed it, and their expectations, quite dramatically. Instead of a familiar and comfortable *homeland*, they discovered that they had returned to a world unfamiliar in many ways: in fact, a *newfoundland*. They had to relearn many things in the age of the internet, jet travel, unimaginable technological innovations—and strikingly changed attitudes toward religious and social morals.

But this is not the whole story, for the erstwhile one-way traffic had become a network of international highways along which people were moving in different directions. People born into rural communities without the amenities of the Western world—electricity, running water, telephones, good roads and transportation systems, and the rest—now found themselves becoming international travelers. And when they too returned home, the contrast between their early formative experiences and the worlds they had encountered far from home often left them in a state of confusion no less easy to resolve than that experienced by those returning to the "civilization" they had left. For everyone, their respective *newfoundland* represented a surprise, a challenge, and unimagined opportunities for sharing the knowledge and experience gained in their *wonderland* with family, peers or parishioners who had never left the *homeland*. New perspectives gleaned from the *wonderland* experience, including new solutions or approaches to common human problems and new ways of dealing with and accommodating "the other," could be a lesson and a boon for their more homebound peers who had little experience of the alternatives and opportunities afforded by living in cross-cultural situations. In short, the contributions of those who have experienced a *wonderland* can enrich the people and parishes of their original *homeland*. They can be of great pastoral benefit to more insular, sedentary, and maintenance-focused communities in a globalized world in desperate need of living creatively with diversity and contributing to the mission of the church, which is in fact an instrument of the eternal *missio Dei*.

If we agree with John Dunne that the "passing over and coming back . . . is the [greatest religious] adventure of our time," then we should ponder the corollary: those without a spirit of adventure and those who do not want to change or be changed, should stay at home lest they do more harm than good.

All this, the potential fruit of a committed cross-cultural person, is extremely pertinent for anyone committed to religious living in today's multicultural world. But we must be even more specific and address the fruits of cross-cultural living in terms of a renewed personal and missionary spirituality.

Spirituality: "A Way of Being in the World with God"

"A way of being in the world with God," or "a Godly way of being in the world," might stand as a convenient description of Christian spirituality in a pluralistic world. But there are surely many ways, states of being, actual worlds, and images or understandings of God, the incomprehensible and ineffable; this range is not only empirically verifiable but in principle consistent with being a particular Christian in a particular context at a particular historical moment. Different though we all are, each of us is called to live a Godly life in our existential situation. And as those situations change—whether due to the natural process of aging and mortality or to the vocational call of each person—so each of us changes and is changed by our circumstances and the grace of conversion. Everyone is different, personally and culturally, yet we are all the same: sharing a common humanity and a common vocation to faithful holiness. And it is in our similarities, and with (not despite) our differences, that we try to live out our personal—yet changing, developing, and maturing—spirituality. The more we encounter other people and other worlds, the more our spirituality is challenged and the more we are called to conversion. The experience of cross-cultural living can be an enormous help and grace in this process.

So how shall we attempt—in our many and varied ways—to do what Jesus did? If we look at the four pillars of the ministry of Jesus, and if we broaden his command "Do this in memory of me" so that it is not confined to the eucharistic liturgy but expanded to include the whole of Jesus' own ministry and everything he did, we can do an examination of conscience and see what challenges lie ahead.

Encounter is the foundation of the ministry of Jesus, as Pope Francis reiterates throughout his apostolic exhortation *Evangelii Gaudium* (3, 7, 264, 269–70, 274). Viktor Frankl affirmed that "to love you must encounter."[4] We cannot love people "in general" because there are no such people, only particular people. And we cannot love "the poor," since that is simply a category, and we cannot love categories, only people. So whom does Jesus encounter, and how? We know the answer: everyone, indiscriminately, but with a preferential option for "the poor"—but one by one, in their specificity. And he is "there" for each person, really present. But how do we measure up? Poorly, indeed. We are selective and often superficial in our encounters, and there is much for us still to do.

Table fellowship is one of the most common pastoral tactics of Jesus: he eats with anyone and everyone, either by inviting himself, being invited, or inviting others. It has been said that this is arguably the main thing that gets Jesus killed.[5] And what of us? We eat with friends, selectively, but do we eat with enemies? Do we go out of our way to turn enemies into friends by table fellowship? Are we friends of the poor? Whom do we avoid and never think of eating with? And whom do we like to be invited by, as an honor and privilege?

Foot washing is of course the central dramatic act in John's Gospel account of the Last Supper. But it is the act, the duty, of a slave, required and never freely undertaken. Jesus freely takes on the role of a slave, shocks the Twelve, and proceeds to demand that they do the same, whether literally or metaphorically. Then he calls them not servants but friends, to remind them that they are not being forced, but that they do have an obligation. We are familiar with the

---

4. Anthony J. Gittins, *A Presence that Disturbs: A Call to Radical Discipleship* (Eugene, OR: Wipf & Stock, 2002), xviii.

5. Robert Karris, *Eating Your Way through Luke's Gospel* (Collegeville, MN: Liturgical Press, 2006).

"scandal" generated by Pope Francis's doing as Jesus did, by his outreach to and inclusion of so many people conventionally seen as "the other," and by his steadfastness in repeating it and then mandating it for the rest of the church. So whose feet do we "wash"? Whose would we never think of washing? Yet who do we expect to "wash" our feet—service workers, menials, low-paid waiters, or hotel maids?

Finally, boundary crossing is much more than leaving one's own cultural world and crossing to another. It entails engaging with whatever margins or boundaries separate us from "the other"—whom we need to encounter by virtue of our call to ministry: cultural, economic, social, religious, or gender-based boundaries, and any other source of separation or alienation. Differences are by no means always to be avoided, and we are required to learn to love, not despite them, but with them whenever and wherever possible.

Jesus is our primary example of some major constituents of authentic cross-cultural ministry. He integrated this ministry through these four constitutive elements. Those who aspire to follow his example must learn to follow in his footsteps. He told the first disciples, and us latter disciples, explicitly: "As I have done, so you should do" (see John 13:15).

Chapter 8

Perspectives from Pope Francis on Priesthood in Religious Life

Robin Ryan, CP

The words and actions of Pope Francis continue to attract the attention of Catholics, other Christians, and people of other religious traditions from around the world. These include his words about the shape of pastoral ministry in the church, including ordained ministry. He has repeatedly challenged bishops and priests to live their vocation with generosity and courage. Many priests find the pope's perspectives on priestly ministry to be refreshing and inspiring. Others seem to wonder if Francis is overly critical in his assessment of the state of priestly ministry in the church.

For a number of reasons, addressing this topic—"Perspectives from Pope Francis on Priesthood in Religious Life"—presents some challenges. First, Francis has not, to my knowledge, presented a systematically developed theology of priesthood. What he says about priestly life and ministry appears to be grounded in the theology found in standard sources like the documents of the Second Vatican Council and Pope St. John Paul II's post-synodal apostolic exhortation *Pastores Dabo Vobis*, as well as his own experience as a Jesuit priest and a bishop. Francis's teaching relates more directly to a spirituality of priestly life and ministry than to a systematic theology of priesthood. Spirituality is, of course, always grounded in some theology, and one can identify salient theological principles and themes that underlie his reflections on the priesthood. Nevertheless, from my research of Francis's writings and talks on priesthood, it appears that he is most interested in addressing the concrete practice of priestly ministry and the everyday life of the priest.

Second, Francis has given most of his talks about priesthood to audiences that include both religious and diocesan priests. Many of these presentations have been reflections or homilies offered at gatherings of priests, seminarians, and members of consecrated life in the various countries he has visited. He has also spoken about priestly life and ministry at the Chrism Masses at which he has presided as bishop of Rome. He has not, to my knowledge, addressed in any extensive way the topic of this conference—the distinctive vocation of religious priesthood. So one has to explore his perspectives on priestly life and ministry in general and then correlate them with priesthood as lived by members of religious communities.

If the ministerial priesthood is meant to serve the priesthood of the faithful—what Vatican II calls the "common priesthood"[1]— then a theology and spirituality of priesthood must be grounded in a theology of church, in ecclesiology. Key dimensions of Pope Francis's ecclesiology can be discerned from his major writings as pope, as well as his homilies and other presentations. In this essay, then, I will reflect on four ecclesiological themes that are prominent in the teaching of Pope Francis. And I will attempt to connect what he says about priestly life and ministry with each of these ecclesiological themes. For Francis, what it means to serve as a priest is directly dependent upon how one understands the nature and mission of the church. The four ecclesiological themes that I will address are the primacy of mercy; communion-in-mission; a church in solidarity with suffering people; and a contemplative church.

The Primacy of Mercy

If you purchase Cardinal Walter Kasper's book *Mercy: The Essence of the Gospel and the Key to Christian Life*, you will find on the cover a quotation from Pope Francis: "This book has done so much good."[2]

---

1. Dogmatic Constitution on the Church (*Lumen Gentium* [LG]), 10.
2. Walter Kasper, *Mercy: The Essence of the Gospel and the Key to Christian Life*, trans. William Madges (New York: Paulist Press, 2014).

As the story goes, Kasper gave Cardinal Bergoglio the recently trans-
lated Spanish edition of his book during the 2013 conclave, and
Bergoglio read it with great interest. In his book, Kasper refers to
the teaching of Thomas Aquinas about mercy in the *Summa Theologiae*. In his discussion of the virtues, Aquinas takes up the question
"Is mercy the greatest of the virtues?" As usual, Aquinas makes the
necessary distinctions, arguing that in one sense charity is the greatest
virtue, since it unites us to God. But he proceeds to teach that "of
all the virtues which have to do with our neighbor . . . mercy is the
greatest." The virtue of mercy entails "giving from one's abundance
to others, and what is more, relieving their needs." Aquinas proceeds
to assert that mercy is "something proper to God and that it is
through mercy, above all, that God shows forth God's almighty
power."[3] In other words, for Aquinas the power of the God who
created this vast and ancient universe is manifested in the most
compelling way in divine mercy.

Pope Francis never seems to tire of talking about divine mercy.
He made this theme the focus of a holy year. In The Joy of the
Gospel, Francis cites the teaching of Aquinas about mercy as the
greatest of the virtues.[4] And in his 2015 message for Lent, he described the season of Lent as a call to each Christian to allow his or
her heart be formed into a merciful heart. A merciful heart, he immediately added, is not a weak heart.[5] To be merciful requires great
inner strength. For Francis, the first and primary word that the
church must speak in its mission of proclaiming the Gospel is the
message about the mercy of God poured out in Jesus Christ. This
word is the heart of the Gospel, and everything else in the Christian
life flows from it. In his homily at the Mass for the possession of the
chair of the bishop of Rome, the pope referred to the parable of the
prodigal son as the "parable of the merciful father," and he observed,
"The son was always in the father's heart, even though he had left
him, even though he had squandered his whole inheritance, his

---

3. Thomas Aquinas, *Summa Theologiae* II-II, q. 30, a. 4, trans. R. J. Batten,
OP, Blackfriars ed., vol. 34, 219–221.

4. Francis, *Evangelii Gaudium* (EG) (The Joy of the Gospel), apostolic
exhortation (Vatican City: Libreria Editrice Vaticana, 2013), 37.

5. Francis, Message for Lent 2015, *Origins* 44, no. 36 (February 12, 2015): 598.

freedom. The father, with patience, love and mercy had never for a second stopped thinking about him."[6] In his apostolic letter for the conclusion of the Year of Mercy, Francis asserted, "Mercy cannot become a mere parenthesis in the life of the church; it constitutes her very existence, through which the profound truths of the Gospel are made manifest and tangible."[7]

Francis's conviction about the primacy of mercy for the mission of the church lies behind one of his most notable and compelling images for the church, that of the "field hospital." He has employed this image repeatedly and in a variety of settings during the past four years. In his 2013 interview with Antonio Spadaro, SJ, Francis mused, "I see clearly that the thing the church needs most today is the ability to heal wounds and to warm the hearts of the faithful. It needs nearness, proximity. I see the church as a field hospital after battle."[8] He constantly expounds the need for pastoral ministers in the church to draw near to the people they serve, to be close to them. Words and phrases that denote nearness, closeness, and proximity are very important to him. And this is because he is convinced of the nearness—the proximity—of God to us, especially when we are hurting or in need. At the 2016 World Youth Day held in Poland, Francis kept assuring the young people of the nearness of God to them.[9]

If mercy constitutes the church's very existence, it must also constitute the very existence of the priest. Pope Francis envisions the priest as someone who has experienced the mercy of God in his own life and who keeps the memory of that experience deep within his heart. In his homily for the 2016 Chrism Mass in Rome, Francis in-

---

6. Francis, Homily at the Mass for the Possession of the Chair of the Bishop of Rome, April 7, 2013, in *The Church of Mercy: A Vision for the Church* (Chicago: Loyola Press, 2014), 4.

7. Francis, *Misericordia et Misera:* Apostolic Letter for the Conclusion of the Year of Mercy, *Origins* 46, no. 27 (December 1, 2016): 417.

8. Francis, "A Big Heart Open to God," interview with Antonio Spadaro, *America* 209, no. 8 (September 30, 2013): 24.

9. See, for example, the homily that Pope Francis gave during the Closing Mass for World Youth Day (July 31, 2016), *Origins* 46, no. 13 (August 11, 2016): 205. Citing the Zacchaeus story in the Gospel of Luke, Francis said, "In other words, Jesus wants to draw near to us personally."

vited the clergy there to remember God's mercy. He said, "Every one of us, looking at our own lives as God does, can try to remember the ways in which the Lord has been merciful toward us, how he has been much more merciful than we imagined."[10] The pope then proceeded to say, "As priests, we are witnesses to and ministers of the ever-increasing abundance of the Father's mercy; we have the rewarding and consoling task of incarnating mercy, as Jesus did."[11] Francis thus envisions the priest as one who has experienced God in his life; the priest is a weak and forgiven sinner who knows that he relies on the mercy of God for everything. From that experience the priest (and every pastoral minister) responds to the call to live and to minister as a sacrament of divine mercy, as a servant who makes the mercy of God palpably present to people in word and deed.

Francis connects this call to mercy with the celebration of the sacraments, especially Eucharist and reconciliation. In The Joy of the Gospel, he asserts that the doors of the sacraments should not be closed for just any reason. Francis observes, "The Eucharist, although it is the fullness of sacramental life, is not a prize for the perfect but a powerful medicine and nourishment for the weak" (EG 47). He laments the fact that priests often seem to act as *arbiters* of sacramental grace rather than as *facilitators* of grace. For Francis, the priest is called to facilitate an encounter between the believer and the God who gives of self in Christ. This conviction seems to underlie his discussion in the eighth chapter of *Amoris Laetitia* about the possibility of forging a path of discernment leading back to the celebration of the sacraments for those who are living in canonically irregular marriage situations.

Francis relates the vocation of the priest to be an icon of divine mercy in a particular way to the sacrament of reconciliation. In the talks that he has given to priests, he speaks about confession frequently and passionately. And his words about confession are grounded in his own personal experience. In his 2016 address to the Missionaries of Mercy—confessors who were commissioned as part

10. Francis, Homily at the Vatican Basilica, Holy Thursday, March 24, 2016, in *Disciples Together on the Road: Words of Pope Francis for Priests* (Washington, DC: USCCB, 2016), 18.

11. Ibid.

of the Year of Mercy—Francis said that "the memory of that confession on September 21, 1953, which redirected my life, is a source of joy for me." He explained that he does not remember what the priest said to him that day. He remembers only that the priest smiled at him and welcomed him like a father.[12] This was a transformative experience that impacted his understanding of his own vocation. This personal experience impels him to underline the importance of the sacrament of reconciliation in the life of the church and to elucidate the posture of compassion that every confessor is called to adopt. The oft-cited passage about reconciliation found in The Joy of the Gospel expresses his conviction in plain language: "I want to remind priests that the confessional must not be a torture chamber but rather an encounter with the Lord's mercy which spurs us on to do our best" (EG 44). He proceeds to teach that "a small step, in the midst of great human limitations, can be more pleasing to God than a life which appears outwardly in order but moves through the day without confronting great difficulties" (44). This comment reflects the Gospel testimony to the public ministry of Jesus, who met people where they were in their lives and brought them to the next step in their journey of faith. Francis even speaks of the duty of the priest-confessor to shield penitents with "the garment of mercy" in order that "they may no longer be ashamed."[13]

Pope Francis's deep conviction about the primacy of the message of divine mercy in the Christian life and in the proclamation of the Gospel colors everything else that he says about the church and pastoral ministry. The enduring mercy of God provides the context for discussion about the mission of the church in the world and the structures that are needed to support that mission. And it serves as the motivating force in the life and ministry of the priest.

12. Francis, Meeting with the Missionaries of Mercy, February 9, 2016, in *Disciples Together on the Road*, 94. In his biography of Pope Francis, Austen Ivereigh chronicles this incident; see *The Great Reformer: Francis and the Making of a Radical Pope* (New York: Henry Holt and Company, 2014), 35–36. Ivereigh quotes a reflection by Pope Francis about this incident in which Francis says, "Right there, I knew I had to be a priest; I was totally certain" (36).

13. Francis, Meeting with the Missionaries of Mercy, February 9, 2016, in *Disciples Together on the Road*, 95.

Communion-in-Mission

In reading and listening to Pope Francis, one often encounters the word "communion." Communion is a foundational building block of his thought in general and certainly of his vision of church. It is connected with his repeated exhortations to promote a "culture of encounter" in the church and throughout the world. It lies at the heart of his understanding of the mystery of God, the human person (theological anthropology), and the nature and mission of the church (ecclesiology).

In his encyclical *Laudato Si'*, Francis emphasizes that the human person has been created for communion. Commenting on the Priestly narrative of creation in Genesis 1, he quotes a passage from the *Catechism of the Catholic Church* that describes the human person as a being who is "capable of self-knowledge, of self-possession and of freely giving himself [herself] and entering into communion with other persons."[14] Francis affirms that "as part of the universe, called into being by one Father, all of us are linked by unseen bonds and together form a kind of universal family, a sublime communion which fills us with a sacred, affectionate and humble respect."[15] He immediately extends the scope of this communion beyond other members of the human family to the rest of creation. In the concluding section of *Laudato Si'*, when he reflects on the mystery of the Trinity, Francis affirms that because the Trinity is the "divine model" for the created world, the world is "a web of relationships." As a partaker of this web of relationships, the human person "grows more, matures more and is sanctified more to the extent that he or she enters into relationships, going out from themselves to live in communion with God, with others and with all creatures."[16] Here readers can perceive the trinitarian foundations of Francis's repeated calls to create a culture of encounter.

---

14. Francis, *Laudato Si'* (On Care for Our Common Home), encyclical letter (Vatican City: Libreria Editrice Vaticana, 2015), 65; *Catechism of the Catholic Church*, 357.
15. *Laudato Si'*, 89.
16. Ibid., 240.

✓   In his reflections on the church, Francis builds on the ecclesiology of communion developed by the Vatican II. At the very beginning of the Dogmatic Constitution on the Church, the council affirmed that the church is "a sacrament—a sign and instrument, that is, of communion with God and of the unity of the entire human race" (LG 1). The council proceeded to teach that the messianic people of God has been established by Christ as "a communion of life, love and truth" (LG 9). In its teaching on episcopal collegiality and on the relationship of the universal church to the particular, or local, churches, Vatican II envisioned the universal church as the communion of particular churches, a worldwide communion of the churches of Chicago, Nairobi, Paris, Manila, and so on.

Communion ecclesiology has been the object of critique by some theologians in recent years, for at least two reasons.[17] Some have observed that in the years after Vatican II communion ecclesiology became focused on hierarchical communion—unity with the hierarchy of the church in faith and life. And they argue that this emphasis obscured and minimized Vatican II's teaching on the church as the people of God. Communion ecclesiology has also been challenged for an excessive concern with the inner life of the church, leading to a neglect of the primacy of mission. Related to this second critique, Stephen Bevans, in an illuminating essay on "missionary ecclesiology," argues, "The challenge of a missionary ecclesiology is to keep a balance between the 'centrifugal' nature of the church lived out in mission and a more 'centripetal' aspect of the church expressed in the understanding of the church as communion. One might characterize the church, as a community of disciples, as a 'communion-in-mission,' a dynamic interplay of communion and mission."[18]

In my view, the ecclesiology of Pope Francis avoids both of the pitfalls that have been adduced by critics of communion ecclesiology.

---

17. See, for example, the essay by Neil Ormerod, "A (Non-*Communio*) Trinitarian Ecclesiology: Grounded in Grace, Lived in Faith, Hope and Charity," *Theological Studies* 76 (September 2015): 448–467.

18. Stephen Bevans, "Beyond the New Evangelization: Toward a Missionary Ecclesiology for the Twenty-First Century," in *A Church with Open Doors: Catholic Ecclesiology for the Third Millennium*, ed. Richard Gaillardetz and Edward Hahnenberg (Collegeville, MN: Liturgical Press, 2015), 3–22, at 14.

Francis articulates a clear understanding of the church as the people of God. As Juan Carlos Scannone points out, Francis was influenced by the *teología del pueblo* developed in Argentina after Vatican II.[19] For example, in The Joy of the Gospel, Francis emphasizes that it is the entire people of God that proclaims the Gospel, and he says that the church "is more than an organic and hierarchical institution; she is first and foremost a people advancing on its pilgrim way to God" (EG 111). With regard to mission, it has become clear that the pope wants to reinvigorate the church with a missionary impetus. His use of the term "missionary discipleship"—borrowed from the 2007 Aparecida document that he helped to draft as archbishop of Buenos Aires—makes that evident. Bevans concludes that what Francis says about mission in The Joy of the Gospel moves the church "toward a vision of the church as going forth as a 'community of missionary disciples.'"[20] Bevans's description of the church as a dynamic interplay of communion and mission is credibly represented in the ecclesiology of Pope Francis.

So if what it means to be church is to be communion-in-mission, the ordained minister, and in fact all pastoral ministers, must become people of communion who are dedicated to the church's mission. The life and ministry of the priest, then, is all about *relationship*, just as we believe that the triune God is all about relationship. The priest is a person who facilitates, nurtures, and builds relationships within the community of disciples and between the church and the wider world. In his 2013 interview with Spadaro, Francis remarked, "I was always looking for community. I did not see myself as a priest on my own. I need a community."[21] He criticizes the tendency to create a "privatized" church, a church confined to our own group or even our own friends. He sees this tendency as selfish and as an expression of the extreme individualism that is so prevalent in western cultures. Reacting to that tendency, he speaks with a sense of urgency: "It is necessary to seek to build communion, to teach communion, to get the better of misunderstandings, starting with the

19. See Juan Carlos Scannone, "El Papa Francisco y la teología del pueblo," *Selecciones de Teología* 54 (2015), 39–50.

20. Bevans, "Beyond the New Evangelization," *A Church with Open Doors*, 10.

21. Francis, "A Big Heart Open to God," 17.

family, with ecclesial reality, in ecumenical dialogue, too. We need reconciliation and communion, and the Church is the home of communion."[22] In his 2014 apostolic letter on consecrated life, Francis addresses this challenge in a particular way to consecrated men and women, calling them to become "experts in communion." He says that in a polarized society consecrated persons "are called to offer a concrete model of community that, by acknowledging the dignity of each person and sharing our respective gifts, makes it possible to live as brothers and sisters."[23]

For Francis, "communion" is really more of a verb than a noun. It is something that we must *do* as people committed to the mission of the church. For the priest, it means first of all that the church must exercise radical hospitality and therefore that the priest is to be a person of gracious welcome. For most religious, the importance of the practice of hospitality is clearly articulated in our constitutions. In our formation as religious, we hear about the virtue of hospitality from prenovitiate onward. Francis drives home the essential importance of creating an atmosphere of welcome in our parishes and other communities—making our faith communities places of hospitality. In an address to newly appointed bishops, he began by urging them to "welcome magnanimously." He said, "May your hearts be large enough to welcome all the men and women you come across during the day and whom you go and seek out when you go about to your parishes and to every community."[24] In a section in The Joy of the Gospel in which Francis adverts to the phenomenon of Catholics' being attracted to fundamentalist churches, he associates this attraction with the sense of a lack of belonging felt by some baptized Catholics. He says that this is due, at least in part, "to certain structures and the occasionally unwelcoming atmosphere of some of our parishes and communities, or to a bureaucratic way of dealing with problems" (EG 63). The pope observes that in many places an *administrative* approach prevails over a *pastoral* approach. Ordained ministers, then, who represent a church

22. Francis, General Audience, November 25, 2013, *The Church of Mercy*, 28.

23. Francis, Apostolic Letter Marking the Start of the Year of Consecrated Life, I, 2, *Origins* 44, no. 29 (December 18, 2014): 483.

24. Francis, Address to Newly Appointed Bishops, September 19, 2013, *The Church of Mercy*, 85.

that is communion-in-mission, are called to be people who master the art of hospitality and who extend a genuine welcome to everyone to whom they minister.

Second, as a person of communion, the priest is called to collaborate with others in the work of ministry, especially with lay women and men. Francis is forceful in his exhortations to clergy to consult and empower the laity. This emphasis is connected with his vision of ministry as accompaniment—*walking with* the people we serve. It is also evident in Francis's stress on the important role of diocesan and parish pastoral councils in discerning the movements of the Spirit. In an address to clergy, religious, and laity gathered in Assisi, Francis observed, "How needed pastoral councils are! A bishop cannot guide a diocese without pastoral councils. A parish priest cannot guide a parish without the parish council."[25] When he met with the clergy and religious of Pennsylvania during his 2015 visit to the United States, Francis noted that "[o]ne of the great challenges facing the Church in this generation is to foster in all the faithful a sense of personal responsibility for the Church's mission, and to enable them to fulfill that responsibility as missionary disciples, as a leaven of the Gospel in our world." He called for more active engagement on the part of the laity, which will necessitate "discerning and employing wisely the manifold gifts which the Spirit pours out upon the Church."[26] Francis added that this collaboration especially entails recognition of the immense contribution that women make to the life of our faith communities. For Francis, a priest is called to be a person of communion in the very exercise of his ministry, one who is willing to share ministry with others. Ordained ministers must empower others to discern and contribute their gifts for the good of the community. It seems to me that religious priests, whose vocations are expressed through a shared life and ministry, are called in a special way to embody this collaborative approach to pastoral ministry.

25. Francis, Meeting with Clergy, Consecrated People and Members of Diocesan Parish Councils, Cathedral of San Rufino, Assisi, October 4, 2013, in *Disciples Together on the Road*, 27.

26. Francis, Mass with Bishops, Priests, and Religious of Pennsylvania, Cathedral of Sts. Peter and Paul, Philadelphia, September 26, 2015, in *Disciples Together on the Road*, 84.

And third, in a church that is communion-in-mission, priests must reach out to those who live on the margins of the church and society. Francis's repeated exhortations to engage the existential and geographical peripheries are well known, and he has modeled this engagement through many symbolic gestures, such as washing the feet of young people at a detention center on Holy Thursday. In a meeting with the parish priests of Rome, the pope reflected on the gospel depictions of Jesus' public ministry, and he posed the question of where Jesus could most easily be found. His answer to that question was "on the road." As he put it, "[Jesus] might have seemed to be homeless, because he was always on the road."[27] For Francis, the priest must "go forth"; he must actively engage the parishioner with a disability who finds it difficult to get to Mass, the woman who sits in the last pew in church because she is in an irregular marriage situation, the homeless person encountered at the soup kitchen who never darkens the door of the church. The priest is called to live "on the road" with the Jesus whose heart was moved with compassion at the sight of the crowds. Priests who are members of consecrated life give witness to their vocation by drawing near to those who live on the margins of this world.

A Church in Solidarity with Suffering People

The call to engage with those who live on the margins of the world brings us to another dimension of Francis's vision of church. Time after time, in a variety of venues, he has taught that the church is called to live in solidarity with others, particularly with the poor and other suffering people. In his homily at the 2016 Chrism Mass, Francis phrased it simply: "As priests, we identify with people who are excluded, people the Lord saves. We remind ourselves that there are countless masses of people who are poor, uneducated, prisoners, who find themselves in such situations because people oppress them."[28] In a homily given to clergy and religious in Manila, Francis

---

27. Francis, Meeting with the Parish Priests of Rome, Paul VI Hall, March 6, 2014, in *Disciples Together on the Road*, 29.

28. Francis, Homily at the Chrism Mass, Vatican Basilica, March 24, 2016, in *Disciples Together on the Road*, 20.

asserted that the Gospel "calls Christian communities to create 'circles of integrity,' networks of solidarity which can expand to embrace and transform society by their prophetic witness."[29]

Francis likes to highlight the poverty of Christ. He cites the verse from Second Corinthians 8:9, where Paul is exhorting the Christians in Corinth to be generous in aiding Jerusalem Christians who are in need. Paul writes, "For you know the gracious act of our Lord Jesus Christ, that for your sake he became poor although he was rich, so that by his poverty you might become rich." In 2007, Pope Benedict XVI cited this same New Testament verse in his opening address to the meeting of the bishops of Latin America and the Caribbean at Aparecida, Brazil. Benedict declared that "the preferential option for the poor is implicit in the Christological faith in the God who became poor for us, so as to enrich us with his poverty."[30] In his Lenten Message for 2014, Pope Francis said, "The poverty of Christ that enriches us is his taking flesh and bearing our weaknesses as an expression of God's infinite mercy to us. The poverty of Christ is the greatest treasure of all."[31]

The fourth chapter of The Joy of the Gospel, which focuses on the social dimension of evangelization, is especially noteworthy for its call to solidarity with the poor. Francis is very direct: "Each individual Christian and every community is called to be an instrument of God for the liberation and promotion of the poor, and for enabling them to be fully part of society" (EG 187). He says that solidarity is a term that is poorly understood; it means more than "a few sporadic acts of generosity." Solidarity entails "the creation of a new mindset which thinks in terms of community and the priority of the life of all over the appropriation of goods by a few" (188). Francis calls for the conversion of both human hearts and economic structures in ways that will generate and effect global solidarity. He exhorts all

29. Francis, Mass with Bishops, Priests and Religious, Cathedral of the Immaculate Conception, Manila, January 16, 2015, in *Disciples Together on the Road*, 63.

30. Benedict XVI, Address to the Bishops of Latin America and the Caribbean, Shrine of Aparecida, May 13, 2007, 3, http://www.vatican.va/holy_father /benedict_xvi/speeches/2007/may/documents/hf_ben-xvi_spe_20070513 _conference-aparecida_en.html.

31. Francis, Lenten Message 2014, *Origins* 43, no. 36 (February 13, 2014): 586.

Christians to think beyond national boundaries to consider the world as a whole: "With due respect for the autonomy and culture of every nation, we must never forget that the planet belongs to all mankind and is meant for all mankind; the mere fact that some people are born in places with fewer resources or less development does not justify the fact that they are living with less dignity" (190).

This shift to a mindset that thinks in terms of community and the priority of the life of all presents distinct challenges for priestly life and ministry. First of all, it requires us to expand our vision beyond our own narrow worlds to encompass the wider world, where so many people live in oppressive situations. While a priest must focus his energies on the particular people he is called to serve, regardless of their socioeconomic status, this more inclusive mindset should always inform his ministry. It may be that this global vision comes more readily to priests who are vowed religious. Most religious priests belong to congregations that extend beyond the particular diocese in which they minister to areas across the world. They are brothers with community members who serve in situations of deprivation and oppression and are in regular communication with them. The fact that three Passionists whom I know well serve in Haiti, helping to run two hospitals and lead other initiatives to benefit very impoverished people, makes me think of Haiti often and pay close attention to news reports about the country. There is a kind of "built-in" solidarity intrinsic to membership in a congregation of consecrated life.

Francis's words about the poverty of Christ also invite us to reflect on the summons to a simple and humble lifestyle. He often observes that the people of God can forgive most any fault of a priest, except if the priest either mistreats people or is attached to money. He is convinced that even diocesan priests, who do not profess a vow of poverty, are called to adopt a simple lifestyle. Speaking to clergy and religious in Nairobi, Francis stated, "In our life as disciples of Jesus, there must be no room for personal ambition, for money, for worldly importance. We follow Jesus to the very last step of his earthly life: the cross."[32] In a dialogue with members of the Union of Superiors

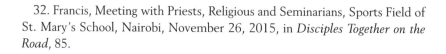

32. Francis, Meeting with Priests, Religious and Seminarians, Sports Field of St. Mary's School, Nairobi, November 26, 2015, in *Disciples Together on the Road*, 85.

General, Francis emphasized the importance of the presence of religious in dioceses and as members of diocesan councils of priests. He asserted that "[a] climate of worldliness and little princes can enter into the structures of the church, and religious have to contribute to destroying this evil climate."[33] Members of religious congregations know well that a religious priest can become just as attached to money as any diocesan priest. Thus, Francis's exhortation to ordained ministers to exemplify a humble and simple lifestyle is a word that must be attended to by both religious and diocesan priests.

I believe that this vision of a church in solidarity with the poor and other suffering people also challenges priests to address principles of social justice in their preaching. It is true that priests must not use the pulpit to engage in partisan politics. And sometimes the line between a clear proclamation of the church's teaching on issues of justice and what sounds like partisan politics is a thin one. But the other extreme—that of avoiding mention of anything that might sound the least bit political—is also problematic. For example, Pope Francis's call to think beyond national boundaries and consider the global situation stands in stark contrast to the "America first" rhetoric that we have recently heard emanating from the halls of Washington. Challenging the narrow, nationalistic vision that is behind such rhetoric is not a matter of partisan politics; it is simply an articulation of the principle of global solidarity that is intrinsic to the Catholic worldview.

A Contemplative Church

The church that is envisioned by Pope Francis is also a contemplative church—a community of disciples whose lives are deeply rooted in prayer and friendship with Jesus Christ. It is customary, of course, for a pope to encourage believers—especially priests—to develop a strong and vibrant prayer life. We would be surprised if we did not hear such exhortations from the pope. Nevertheless, my study of

33. Francis, Meeting with the Union of Superiors General, Paul VI Hall, November 25, 2016, https://www.ncronline.org/news/vatican/pope-admits -corruption-vatican-wide-ranging-talk-men-religious.

Pope Francis's writings leaves me with the impression that this contemplative dimension of ecclesial life has a place of particular importance in his vision of the church and of ministry within the church. When he stood on the balcony after his election and asked for the blessing of the people prior to giving his own papal blessing, one was left with the sense that this is someone who knows the importance of prayer. His formation as a Jesuit, rooted in the *Spiritual Exercises* of Ignatius of Loyola, is a principal source of his contemplative spirit. We should not be surprised that a pope formed by the *Exercises* speaks so often of the importance of discernment.

Pope Francis's teaching about the contemplative dimension of the church is grounded in his vision of God and his conviction about the primacy of grace in the life of the church and of every believer. There is a very striking sentence in a reflection on the spirituality of Guadalupe that he offered during his 2016 meeting with the bishops of Mexico. Francis simply said: *"The need for familiarity abides in the heart of God."* Strictly speaking, a dogmatic theologian acquainted with the tradition of classical theism represented by theologians like Augustine of Hippo and Thomas Aquinas might well object to that statement. According to classical Christian theology, God has no needs; God does not need anything or anyone. Both the creation of the universe and God's call to human beings to live in covenant relationship with God are pure gifts. They are not initiatives undertaken by God to fulfill some unmet needs in God. Rather, they are acts of pure benevolence. I suspect that Pope Francis would affirm this traditional teaching if asked to do so. Nevertheless, Francis appears to envision the God who has self-revealed in Jesus Christ to be the God who spontaneously, and even inevitably, draws close. God is the familiar God; God is even the humble God, who drew near in the child who was born in a barn. In this vein, one is reminded of Karl Rahner's reflections on grace and incarnation, rooted in the Franciscan theological tradition represented especially by Duns Scotus. Rahner argued that, while creation and the gift of grace are free gifts of God, the Christian can conclude from the way in which God has self-revealed that what was "on God's mind" from the very beginning was the desire to give of self in love. God created the world and the human family in order to have a recipient of God's self-communication. God passionately desired to enter into personal union with God's beloved—that is, with us. Ultimately, that is the reason there is anything at all; that is why there is something, and not nothing. That is the logic at the heart of the universe.[34]

At the same time, Pope Francis also underlines the gratuity of grace in our life with God. Francis tries to hold these two insights together in a kind of creative tension: the need for familiarity abides in the heart of God; yet God's gift of self to us is a purely gratuitous gift. It is a gift that makes a positive response on our part possible. Francis is keenly aware that the life of the church—the Christian life—is first and foremost a response. It is a response to the faithful, tenacious love of God poured out in Jesus Christ. The Christian life is not akin to "spiritual Olympic training" through which we find our way to the distant God by mastering exercises of spiritual discipline. It is a response to God's gracious initiative in our lives. Francis likes to quote the First Letter of John on this point: "In this way the love of God was revealed to us: God sent his only Son into the world so that we might have life through him. In this is love: not that we have loved God, but that he loved us and sent his Son as expiation for our sins" (1 John 4:9-10). And so, near the beginning of The Joy of the Gospel, Francis says, "The life of the Church should always reveal clearly that God takes the initiative, that 'he has loved us first' (1 John 4:19) and that he alone 'gives the growth' (1 Cor 3:7)" (12). Francis exhorts every Christian, especially priests and consecrated people, to make memory of the initiative of God's grace in their lives. They must be mindful of the many mysterious ways in which God has reached out to them and touched their lives. In a meeting with priests and religious in Ecuador, Francis said, "Two principles for you who are priests and consecrated persons: every day renew the conviction that everything is a gift, the conviction that your being chosen is gratuitousness—we do not merit it—and every day ask for the grace not to forget your memories, and not to fall into self-importance."[35]

34. Karl Rahner, "Concerning the Relationship between Nature of Grace," *Theological Investigations*, vol. 4: *More Recent Writings*, trans. Kevin Smyth (London: Darton, Longman & Todd, 1968), 310.

35. Francis, Meeting with Priests, Religious and Seminarians, National Marian Shrine of "El Quinche," Quito, Ecuador, July 8, 2015, in *Disciples Together on the Road*, 67.

It is within this overarching context of the familiarity of God and of God's gracious initiative in our lives that Pope Francis speaks about the importance of the regular practice of prayer. In The Joy of the Gospel, he emphasizes that the evangelizing work of the church must be fueled and sustained by prayer. He observes, "What is needed is the ability to cultivate an interior space which can give a Christian meaning to commitment and activity" (EG 262). Francis employs strong language to make his point: "Without prolonged moments of adoration, of prayerful encounter with the word, of sincere conversation with the Lord, our work easily becomes meaningless: we lose energy as a result of weariness and difficulties, and our fervor dies out" (EG 262). Francis does not think that anything done in the service of the Lord is ever meaningless. But it is the case that without regular encounter with the Lord in prayer, we can easily lose our focus and lose touch with the true motivation that should be guiding our endeavors. Speaking to diocesan priests, Francis asserts that the diocesan priest must be a contemplative priest, though not in the same way that a Carthusian is called to practice contemplation. He says, "The priest must have contemplativeness, an ability to contemplate both God and people."[36] In other words, the priest—diocesan or religious—is called to be a person who *pays attention*. The priest must give sustained attention to God in prayer and sustained attention to the aspirations, concerns, and needs of the people he serves.

Francis tells priests that the experience and practice of prayer is a primary source of creativity in the church. He points to the creativity of the early Christian community, under the guidance of the Holy Spirit, in coming to terms with its relationship with Judaism, as represented by Paul in his outreach to Gentiles and Peter in his inspired visit to the house of Cornelius (Acts 10). Francis claims that if the priest wishes to be creative in the Spirit "there is no other way than prayer."[37] Prayer is, in the mind of Francis, the condition for the church's moving forward in its mission to the world. It is the deepest source of creativity for the church in advancing the reign of God.

36. Francis, Meeting with the Priests of the Diocese of Caserta, Palatine Chapel in the Royal Palace of Caserta, July 26, 2014, in *Disciples Together on the Road*, 49.

37. Ibid., 46.

I find the words about prayer that Francis originally addressed to a group of catechists gathered in Rome to be particularly intriguing. Francis told the catechists a story about a young man who had come up to him and explained that, while he was very glad to meet the pope, he did not have the gift of faith. The pope did not berate him or chide him for his lack of faith. Rather, he urged this young man not to become discouraged, and he assured him of God's love. Then he suggested that the young man should let himself be gazed upon by God. Francis proceeded to say to the catechists, "And this is the same thing I would say to you: let yourselves be gazed at by the Lord!"[38] He spoke similar words to a group of priests about prayer before the Blessed Sacrament: "When we priests are before the tabernacle, and we pause there for a moment, in silence, we then feel Jesus' gaze upon us once more; this gaze renews us, reinvigorates us."[39] Francis's advice to allow ourselves to be gazed upon by the Lord reflects his vision of a church, and the life of a priest, that is contemplative.

Those of us who are committed to consecrated life belong to congregations that attempt to integrate the demands of contemplation and apostolic activity. This integration is expressed differently in the various constitutions of our communities, and it is exemplified in diverse ways by the founders and other significant figures in the history of our congregations. It remains an abiding challenge for all of us. We never seem to come upon the precise "formula" that will secure this integration of the contemplative and the apostolic for the duration of our lives as consecrated persons. Pope Francis, from his own experience as a Jesuit priest and his ministry as a bishop, is quite aware of the difficulty of this synthesis of the contemplative and the apostolic, especially in the fast-paced world in which we live. He grapples with this integration in his own life as bishop of Rome. Francis's words and example, however, speak in a credible way to religious priests about the urgent need to root our active ministry in a vibrant and disciplined life of prayer. Each of us is called

38. Francis, Address to the Participants at the International Congress on Catechesis, September 27, 2013, *The Church of Mercy*, 16.
39. Francis, Speech Prepared by the Holy Father and Given during the Meeting with Diocesan Priests of the Cathedral (Cassano all'Jonio), June 21, 2014, in *Disciples Together on the Road*, 36.

to make our lives an ongoing conversation with God—the God who draws close, who has a "need" for familiarity.

Conclusion

For Francis, the church is a sacrament of divine mercy; it is communion-in-mission; it is a community of believers who cultivate solidarity with people who are suffering; and it is a contemplative church. These four dimensions of Francis's ecclesiology do not exhaust his vision of church; his ecclesial vision is richer and more expansive than I have been able to address in this essay. But these four dimensions are, I believe, central to his vision of what the church is and what it is called to be.

Francis invites all priests to respond to the challenges inherent in this vision of church. As religious priests, we are to keep the memory of the mercy God bestowed on us in calling us to religious life. We are challenged to enable others to experience God's mercy in their lives. As religious priests, we are summoned to allow our experience of communion-in-mission within religious community to inform our ministry in the church. Since the triune God is all about relationship, we are called to foster a culture of encounter within the church and between the church and the wider world. As religious priests, we are called to allow the solidarity with suffering people across the globe that we experience in our congregations to inform our service to the people of God. We must strive to internalize within ourselves and to inspire in others a genuine concern for the many people who struggle to survive. And as religious priests, we are challenged to engage the contemplative traditions found within our communities and to share our experience of prayer with the people to whom and with whom we minister. We are invited to witness to the God in whose heart abides the need for familiarity.

Chapter 9

An African American Perspective
of Priesthood in Religious Life

Maurice J. Nutt, CSsR

> *Done made my vow to the Lord,*
> *And I never will turn back,*
> *Oh, I will go, I shall go*
> *To see what the end will be.*
>
> *Sometimes I'm up; sometimes I'm down;*
> *See what the end will be,*
> *But still my soul is heav'nly bound,*
> *See what the end will be. (Refrain)*
> —*Done Made My Vow,* African American Spiritual

> *You did not choose me but I chose you. And I appointed you to go and bear fruit, fruit that will last, so that the Father will give you whatever you ask him in my name.*
> —John 15:16; NRSV

On July 24, 1983, the Scripture passage cited above was the text that my profession class chose for the gospel proclaimed at our Mass of religious profession as Redemptorists. While this Scripture text was deemed appropriate for our eucharistic liturgy so many years ago, I have come to a greater appreciation of the meaning of this text in my vowed consecrated life and priesthood. I have realized that no matter the situation or circumstance I have encountered as a religious priest, it is not about me—meaning my likes, dislikes, concerns, or

137

preferences—but about God, who chose me to witness to the Gospel of Jesus Christ and to serve the people of God through my religious vows and my sacramental priesthood. As a member of the Congregation of the Most Holy Redeemer, I was chosen to give my life in service to preaching the Gospel to the poor and most abandoned. I was chosen to minister where others may not choose to go. I was chosen to give my life for plentiful redemption by living Good News and being Good News in a world that often experiences bad news. It is important for me both to understand that, for whatever reason, God has chosen me, with my faults and frailties as well as my strengths and abilities, as an instrument of God in the world and to remain faithful even in difficult moments and those times when I think that being chosen is too great a burden to accept or endure.

The focus of my priestly ministry as a religious priest is grounded in my vowed religious life. Considering what attracted me to my vocation, I recall that the most alluring aspects of my calling were not necessarily found in church or in the sanctuary. I was reared in a Redemptorist parish. Even at an early age, I accepted my eventual liturgical and sacramental ministry as part and parcel of my priesthood. However, I was drawn to the community life and prayer life of the Redemptorists. Somehow, I instinctively knew that communal interactions and relationships, along with a well-grounded communal and personal prayer life, were foundational to the ministry of the Redemptorists. I was equally drawn to their closeness to the people they served. They did not stay cooped up behind the walls of the rectory. I witnessed them walking the streets of our inner-city housing project. They visited our homes, sat on our porches or at our kitchen tables, were joyful and "down-to-earth"; we knew that they sincerely cared about us. While my family was Catholic, they not only showed care and concern for the Catholics, but were also compassionate toward all the people of our neighborhood. It was fascinating seeing these white men, many times in clerical garb or their religious habits, freely walking through the housing project even at night. My mother would often remark that they had to be either holy or crazy to walk our inner-city streets at night. But they had nothing to fear; besides having God with them, they also garnered the esteem and respect of everyone. There was a sense in the greater community that these were *our* Catholic priests and brothers! I was also enthralled by their commitment to work for the poor and to seek justice. It was not unusual to see a Redemptorist at city hall protesting unfair hiring and employment policies of the city or attending community meetings to advocate for better housing conditions for the poor or improvements within the neighborhood. I would later learn that these men were missionaries, and missionaries are sent—they go out to seek the lost, the neglected, and the marginalized. Yes, I witnessed them celebrate Mass, preach homilies, and administer the sacraments, but the unintentional vocation promotion that called me to this religious congregation was their preaching to the poor and abandoned, not just from the pulpit but by the persuasive witness of their lives.

But They Don't Look Like Me

I knew as early as seven years old that I wanted to be a Redemptorist priest. The Redemptorists fascinated me when I was growing up. My father died when I was three years old. While I had older brothers and a host of uncles, one Redemptorist priest, Fr. Joseph Campbell, stepped into my life, and I remember wanting to do what he did and to become the kind of man that he was.

Fr. Campbell was the pastor of my home parish when I was child. Besides being an altar server, I found myself hanging around the church a lot. I would go with him to visit the sick in hospitals, visit the elderly, and take food to the poor. Fr. Campbell seemed always joyful and content with his priestly life and ministry. He was extremely generous with his time and resources. As a pastor, he had time for the young and old alike. He taught me how to swim and how to play basketball; he also taught me how to serve Mass and to pray the rosary. Everyone in the parish would call me Fr. Campbell's son, and I wore that moniker as a badge of honor. In fact, since his full name was Joseph Thomas Campbell and my baptismal name was Joseph, at confirmation I chose the name Thomas so that I could be known as Maurice Joseph Thomas Nutt.

I remember the happiness I felt at my First Holy Communion when I received the eucharistic presence of Jesus at the hands of Fr. Campbell for the first time. I remained in contact with him after he was transferred from our parish. He attended my high school and college graduations and even vested me as a priest at my ordination. As providence would have it, I was the one to offer him the Anointing of the Sick and preach at his funeral Mass when God called him home. This gregarious and gentle Irish-American priest meant the world to me.

I had never seen an African American[1] priest at that time. There was another young black man from our parish who was inspired by Fr. Campbell to become a Redemptorist priest. He was ordained ten years before me; his name was Charles Brown. The very first black priest from my parish, Fr. Wendell Sams, CSsR, was ordained in 1963. Fr. Sams left the priesthood in the late sixties during the height of the Civil Rights movement. I met Wendell Sams years later; he confessed that he left because the Redemptorists were not ready to accept a "self-determined black man," meaning a black man who refused to fully assimilate into the dominant white culture. Three years after I entered the high school seminary formation program with the Redemptorists, Charles Brown was ordained a Redemptorist priest. His ordination was the impetus I needed to know that, I, too, could one day reach my goal of becoming a religious priest. Fr. Brown was not only a black Redemptorist priest but he later taught me philosophy in the college seminary. I was saddened that a few years after my own ordination, for various reasons Fr. Brown found it difficult to persevere in his vocation as a Redemptorist priest and left—leaving me to this day as the sole African American Redemptorist priest in my Province.

Assimilation: Denying Who You Are

Merriam-Webster defines the word "assimilation" to mean:

1. a: an act, process, or instance of assimilating. b: the state of being assimilated.

2. the process of receiving new facts or of responding to new situations in conformity with what is already available to consciousness.

1. While it most common to use the term "African American" in making reference to those in America of the African diaspora, for purposes of this work "black" and "African American" are used interchangeably.

For purposes here, I use the word "to assimilate" to mean to try to fit in or be accepted. Entering a high school minor seminary program at the age of thirteen, I was admittedly idealistic and naïve. Coming from an inner-city parish where the all-white missionaries not only accepted our African American culture but also embraced the beauty and dignity of "blackness," I expected this to be the case among my classmates. While most of the students at the high school seminary were friendly, I am now keenly aware that they were friendly because I extended myself to fit into their reality and cultural life experiences. My extending or stretching myself was my way of seeking acceptance and essentially validation.

In seminaries and houses of formation, the dominant culture is so pervasive that it allows for no deviation from what is considered the norm. An African American seminarian lives in a building where none of the artwork looks like him; the food that is served is sometimes unfamiliar and lacks flavor and seasoning; and the popular music that the seminarians enjoy and television shows that they like to watch are not appealing. Familiar cultural idioms or expressions are not the norm and are deemed unacceptable. Inappropriate comments and racial insensitivity are common in most seminaries and houses of formation. When rude and hurtful comments are made, the African American seminarian will not inform the perpetrator that what was said is degrading and inconsiderate but will simply endure it, not wanting to create a hostile environment or to be rejected. At times, the African American seminarian will even laugh at the racially degrading comment—again, to fit in and to be accepted. For many African Americans, seminary formation is a rite of passage where they think to themselves: If I can just get through this period and become a fellow religious or priest, then perhaps they will accept me for who I am and acknowledge the gifts that I bring as an equal.

The Need for Cultural Affirmation

African American seminarians and priests have an intrinsic need to have their culture respected and affirmed. Historically, seminaries, houses of formation, and the parishes where priests were assigned have not culturally been places of welcome and affirmation. The environment and atmosphere does not say that someone of a specific culture even lives in this place! I am not speaking of superficial, patronizing images or artifacts that have no authentic meaning to the person but rather something that perhaps they personally would want included in the place where they live, study, or work. When I visit formation houses or seminaries and look at the artwork, you would never know that a person who is Latino/a, African (Caribbean, Afro-Latino, African American), or Asian (from various cultures) lives there. When questioned, the superior would quip, "We have normal [or the standard] religious artwork displayed." This implies that anything germane to a specific culture outside of the dominant culture could be interpreted as abnormal and could never be considered the standard. Symbols speak. They speak to a reality of exclusion.

Cultural inclusion and affirmation for the African American priest in religious life certainly goes beyond artwork to include music (sacred and secular), foods that are culturally traditional and comforting, and the ability to wear cultural attire without negative comments or criticism. While we all are called to make personal sacrifices when entering religious life, I firmly believe that when accepting the charism of a religious order one does not have to forfeit one's cultural identity. In fact, one should share one's cultural identity as gift to the religious community and to the greater church. Cultural affirmation within priesthood and religious life goes far beyond simply being polite or respectful; for the African American priest or religious, it is an inherent sociopsychological necessity. Furthermore, to deny someone access to and affirmation of their cultural or ethnic identity could be viewed as devaluing the doctrine of the incarnation. Christians believe that in the incarnation, God assumed the limitations of human existence and a particular culture. The failure to affirm a person's cultural identity minimizes the importance of God's creating humanity in God's own image and likeness. Who we are, save sin, is a mirror of the God we love and serve.

The Need for Cultural Community

But the reality is that one religious community cannot meet the cultural needs of African American religious priests. It simply cannot.

I remember being strongly invited by the other African American/ African Caribbean Redemptorists to go to a joint conference of black priests, deacons and their wives, religious women and men, and seminarians. I didn't know such groups existed, and after all, I somehow thought that when I became a religious that I was a religious first and African American second. But I went anyway. It happened that in 1984 the joint conference of the National Black Catholic Clergy Caucus, the National Black Sisters Conference, the National Association of Black Catholic Deacons (and their wives), and the National Black Catholic Seminarians Association was meeting in New Orleans. The conference would culminate with the first commencement of the Institute for Black Catholic Studies (IBCS) at Xavier University of Louisiana, where three students (two black sisters and a white diocesan priest) would receive their master of theology degrees. Sr. Thea Bowman, FSPA, a faculty member of the IBCS, was the commencement speaker. She spoke passionately about the gifts and giftedness of black Catholics and what we bring to the church universal. I received an epiphany that evening. I realized that black priests, black religious, and black Catholic laity alike all desperately needed formation into what it meant to be black and Catholic. I felt like Sr. Thea was speaking directly to me. It was a cathartic moment. I needed to experience spiritual and cultural formation and intellectual inquiry to be deemed whole and holy as an African American religious priest. I entered the very next cohort of the IBCS in the summer of 1985 even before entering the Master of Divinity program at Catholic Theological Union in Chicago that fall. Several other seminarians from a number of religious communities entered the program as well.

Founded in 1980, the Institute for Black Catholic Studies at Xavier University of Louisiana offers programs in pastoral theology, religious education, and pastoral ministry. The IBCS provides an intellectual, spiritual, and cultural immersion in the black Catholic experience for all those interested in or committed to Catholic ministry within the black community. The IBCS is a response to Pope Paul VI's 1969 homiletic admonition to the Catholic bishops of Africa to formulate Catholicism in terms congenial to their own culture. It is essentially a "school that meets in the summer." Rigorous yet exhilarating, the intensive three-week summer session focuses on assisting those engaged in or preparing to engage in highly effective ministry in multicultural and multiracial parishes. Being formed, inspired, and encouraged in my black identity and spirituality through the IBCS changed the trajectory of my self-awareness and ultimately my ministry. In the words of Sr. Thea Bowman, I could proudly claim being my beloved "black self" while serving as a religious priest within the Catholic Church: "I bring myself, my black self, all that I am, all that I have, all that I hope to become. I bring my whole history, my traditions, my experience, my culture, my African American song and dance and gesture and movement and teaching and preaching and healing and responsibility as gift to the Church."[2]

African American Spirituality

It is imperative for a well-formed African American religious priest not only to be cognizant of but also to be able to "live out" his cultural spirituality. Being able to fully and freely function within the context of my African American spirituality has brought me the graces of solace, serenity, and strength throughout my priestly sojourn. Spirituality is faith lived. As such, it encompasses the totality of personal and collective responses to religious belief, including relationships, morality, worship, and daily living. As Christians, we strive to understand and to act in a way that makes us part of the reality that is the will and purpose of God. Thus, black spirituality is "pervaded with the African American experience and awareness."[3] It is at once a response to and a reflection on African American life and culture. It is rooted in African heritage and religious traditions through its ways of perceiving and valuing reality, its style of expression, and its modes of prayer and of contemplating the divine. It is colored by the experiences of the Middle Passage, slavery, the Caribbean and Latin experience, segregation, integration, and African Americans' ongoing

---

2. Thea Bowman in *Sister Thea Bowman, Shooting Star: Selected Writings and Speeches*, ed. Celestine Cepress, FSPA (Winona, MN: St. Mary's Press, 1993), 32.

3. Cyprian Davis, OSB, "The Black Contributions to a North American Spirituality," *New Catholic World* 225 (July–August, 1982), 184.

struggle for justice and liberation. It is expressed in every geographic locale, whether urban or rural, Southern, Northern, Eastern, or Western. It is present in every socioeconomic level—rich, middle-class, and poor. Black spirituality is influenced by present experiences and those of African American forebears, not only in the Catholic Church but in other churches as well. It bears elements from staunch high churches to Spirit-filled, hand-clapping, foot-stomping storefront churches. African American spirituality is clearly identified as biblical, communal, contemplative, joyful, and holistic in nature.[4] Regardless of the circumstances, wherever African Americans have sought to find meaning, purpose, identity, community, worth, and God together, black spirituality has grown and flourished. Black spirituality, in the final analysis, offers a keen sense of the omniscience of God, who is ever-present. It is embodied in the black idiom of the elders, who often fervently exclaimed, "If it had not been for the Lord on my side, where would I be?"

The Grace of Perseverance

While priestly vocational perseverance is not reserved to any one cultural group, I have found that being African American in the midst of the dominant European-American religious communities offers unique challenges. Outside of the cultural and spiritual differences, when living in religious communities there is a belief among many African American religious priests that although you will certainly experience both covert and overt racist comments, attitudes, and ideologies, you should persevere. Many African American religious priests understand that their call to priesthood in religious life is much bigger than themselves. Most religious communities in the United States have few if any vocations from among African Americans. The fact that African American religious priests have persevered through isolating and at times debilitating circumstances is a testament that they are not only called by God but called from the African American community to serve that community's needs as

4. African American Catholic Bishops, *What We Have Seen and Heard* (Cincinnati: St. Anthony Messenger Press, 1984), 5.

well. Black people send their sons to religious communities with an expectation that they will garner the fruit of their prayers and sacrifices and will have black priests to serve in their local parishes. This is not an unfounded or unrealistic expectation. There have been moments when I have questioned my vocation, when I have experienced loneliness being the only African American among my mostly white brothers, when the vowed life seemed too imposing and demanding and I simply wanted to leave—when I wanted to leave, but God would not let me go. This experience is common, but somehow, at least for me, I know that God called me and supplies the grace to persevere. A strong prayer life, spiritual direction, making an annual retreat, utilizing the sacrament of reconciliation, reading spiritual and cultural books, appreciating African American cultural expressions (music, dance, theatre, art), and remaining closely connected to the African American community, especially other black priests and religious, all sustain my priesthood in religious life.

The Unique Ministry of African American Religious Priests

Ecumenical Ministry

Most African Americans come from diverse religious backgrounds. In some geographic locations in the United States where the black Catholic demographic is large, like Louisiana and Maryland, many African Americans converted to Catholicism. Therefore, some of their relatives belong to Baptist, Methodist, Presbyterian, Episcopal, or Pentecostal denominations. It has been vital for me to be able to minister ecumenically. Within the black community, there is an expectation of a black priest that while you may be Catholic by faith, you should be able to interconnect predominantly African American denominations. Here again, I am grateful for my IBCS training because it gave me the capacity to meet this ecumenical expectation. As a black priest, I was confident in my knowledge of African American religious history, song, and prayer and preaching expressions. It has allowed me to minister to family members of other denominations and to work with various pastors and congregations on local community issues.

Social and Racial Justice Issues

Without equivocation, I became a priest to serve the poor, the oppressed, the marginalized, disenfranchised, and neglected. Biblical admonitions, Catholic social teaching, the wisdom of the Second Vatican Council, and papal encyclicals are impetus for the work of peace and justice. My call to serve as a religious priest is inseparable from the gospel mandate to care for the "least of these" (Matt 25:40; NRSV). Given the tumultuous history that African Americans have had to endure, including slavery, Jim Crow segregation, police brutality, the civil rights movement, and the current resurgence of white supremacists, racism, and bias, the black community looks to their religious leaders for consolation, counsel, and a fervent commitment to advocacy and activism. In my estimation, black Catholic religious priests cannot negate their responsibility to be advocates and activists for peace and justice.

I disdain empty rhetoric; that's why I try to "practice what I preach" in regard to issues of justice and equality. In a 1961 speech, the Rev. Dr. Martin Luther King Jr. stated: "Human progress is neither automatic nor inevitable. . . . Every step toward the goal of justice requires sacrifices, suffering, and struggle; the tireless exertions and passionate concern of dedicated individuals."[5] Traditional black congregations have looked to their ministers to advocate on their behalf for civil rights. I believe that the quest for justice and equality should be in the moral fiber of an African American Catholic priest. It was not until the early twentieth century that African American men were allowed to prepare for the Roman Catholic priesthood in the United States. The first recognized African American Catholic priest serving in the United States was Fr. Augustus Tolton (1854–1897). Tolton, born into slavery in Missouri, escaped to Illinois to freedom with his mother and two siblings.[6] He had to travel to Rome to prepare for the priesthood and was ordained there in 1886. Tolton was originally preparing to be a missionary

5. Martin Luther King Jr. speech made at New York University's former University Heights campus in the Bronx, February 10, 1961.

6. Cyprian Davis, *The History of Black Catholics in the United States* (New York: Crossroad, 1990), 153.

priest on the continent of Africa until divine providence and a wise prelate, Cardinal Simeoni, decided otherwise.[7] Peter Joseph Baltes, bishop of Alton (now Springfield, Illinois), agreed to accept Fr. Tolton as a priest of his diocese.[8] Because of his unbearable suffering and valiant courage and persistence in the face of blatant racism, Fr. Tolton's cause for canonization is in process. The first black priest ordained in the United States was Josephite father Charles Randolph Uncles in 1891 in Baltimore.[9] Missionaries of the Society of the Divine Word, recognizing and combatting injustice, as well as acknowledging the humanity and equality of African Americans and knowing the urgent pastoral needs of the black community, fearlessly opened the first seminary for African American men in 1920 in Greenville, Mississippi; the seminary later moved to Bay St. Louis, Mississippi.[10] And even after receiving the sacrament of holy orders, black priests encountered the reluctance of many (arch)dioceses to accept them. Knowing the insidious obstacles and opposition to the descendants of the African diaspora serving the church as priests (both religious and secular) should compel black Catholic priests to vehemently confront and seek to eradicate racism in society and in the church. Our religious and priestly identities and existence are commingled with the pursuit of justice and equality.

Unfortunately, race continues to be a factor that separates and wounds the Body of Christ today. As the church in America continues to become increasingly black and brown; as priests from far-flung places throughout the globe come to minister to Catholic Americans; as Eucharist is celebrated in English by men with accents at times difficult to understand: we must surrender to the reality that *we* are now the missionary church. The matter of race can no longer be ignored or fantastically wished away. There has been set forth a clarion call for racial acceptance, not merely tolerance—racial healing and racial reconciliation. While black and brown religious priests in solidarity with their particular ethnic groups are undeniably the objects of racism, I believe that as "wounded healers," we are in the

7. Ibid.,155.
8. Ibid.
9. Ibid., 262.
10. Ibid., 234.

unique position not only to oppose racist behavior but also to create opportunities to banish ignorance through conversations and commitment to racial harmony and equality.

Realizing and accepting the complexities, challenges, and moments of sublime happiness as a religious priest, I remain resolute in my conviction that I *"done made my vow to the Lord and I never will turn back."*

## Chapter 10

Prophetic Priesthood: Latinx Narratives

Eddie De León, CMF

> *Once social change begins, it cannot be reversed.*
> *You cannot un-educate the person who has learned to read.*
> *You cannot humiliate the person who feels pride.*
> *You cannot oppress the people who are not afraid anymore.*
> —César Chávez

Good stories are at the heart of good preaching, and good preaching is a necessary dimension of prophetic priesthood. For Puerto Ricans, stories nurture identity—cuentos about our familias, about nuestra gente, about our people. For Latinx in the United States, our stories of resistance shape our prophetic responses to experiences of exclusion and marginalization.[1] As the son of diasporic parents from Puerto Rico, cuentos rooted me in a larger family story over two thousand miles away and in the migrant struggles of my parents and grandparents. As a child growing up in East Chicago, Indiana, the stories told through the movies that my mother loved captivated my imagination. As a Latinx preacher and teacher of preaching, I draw from this wealth of narratives—from my familia, from the struggles of mi gente, and from my passion for films—to make sense of what it means for priesthood to be prophetic.

---

1. I use the terms Latinx, Latino/a, and Hispanic interchangeably to reference the diverse communities that fall under the broad constructs of hispanidad y latinidad in the United States.

Mi Familia, A Story of Diaspora

As the plane from San Juan, Puerto Rico, landed in Chicago's Midway Airport, thunderous applause erupted. "Welcome to Chicago," said the pilot. My mom remembers the details to this day. She wore a yellow dress with her hair up in a ponytail. She was ten, accompanied by her mother and three sisters. My grandmother would no longer be working at a cigar factory in Caguas. My mom was finally going to see her papi, mi abuelo, who had arrived well in advance in order to secure work, housing, and a Catholic parish. They had all thought that this reunion day would never come. They had waited such a long time. After some tears and long awaited abrazos y besos at the airport, they searched for their luggage, which my mom likes to tell me was merely rope-tied cardboard boxes with handles. In their luggage was everything they owned: clothing, kitchen plates, household items, and, yes, un caldero. Everything else had been sold, including their house, to the parish priest, who planned to use it as an extension of the church for catechism classes. The year was 1948, the continuation of the diaspora of mi familia begun by my grandfather. As with count-less Puerto Rican migrants from their generation, Noel Estrada's nostalgic anthem echoed their loss and longing.

> En mi Viejo San Juan
> cuantos sueños forjé
> en mis noches de infancia. . .
> Adios (adios, adios)
> Borinquen querida (tierra de mi amor).[2]

Their journey from Puerto Rico through Midway Airport ended in East Chicago, Indiana, after a forty-five minute car ride. East Chicago was a steel city and a small intercultural community. My mom's new neighborhood consisted of a mix of Mexican, Puerto Rican, African American, and white neighbors. There she joined my abuelo as well as the man who would become my father.

Years earlier, mi papa and my abuelo had met each other in Utah, where good work and great pay were being offered to men from Puerto

2. Noel Estrada, "En mi Viejo San Juan," RCA Victor, 1943.

Rico. Puerto Ricans were American citizens, and that made hiring less complicated for employers; however, these men were taken advantage of just like many immigrants today. While they were US citizens, most did not speak English and could not defend their rights or themselves in a land they experienced as a foreign country. One night my dad convinced my grandfather and others to make a run for it and leave the mines of Utah, most probably uranium mines, which boomed in the 1940s and '50s. During this time, my dad recounted, they were all afraid of what would happen to them if they were caught, but they recognized the fact that they were being treated more like slaves than citizens. So, they ran as fast and as far as they could, which brought them to northwest Indiana. After securing new work and a place to live, they sought the refuge of the Catholic Church and its priests, something that they had been comfortable doing in Puerto Rico. Their luck had changed for the better, and they were well on their way in pursuit of the "American Dream." Our Lady of Guadalupe was their new parish, and in the future it would be the place where their children would receive all of their sacraments, where our family would celebrate weddings and funerals, and where as a newly ordained priest I would preside at my Mass of thanksgiving.

Stories of Exclusion and Prophetic Resistance

Many Catholic immigrants from Europe arrived in the United States accompanied by their own clergy or welcomed into national parishes where they would encounter ministry in their familiar home cultures and languages. This was not the case for many Mexican Americans, Mexican immigrants, and Puerto Rican migrants. This vacuum left them more vulnerable to injustices and mistreatment. Each Latinx community has its own complicated history, struggles with marginalization, as well as stories of prophetic resistance. What follows is not intended to be comprehensive; rather it offers a window into the complexity and diversity of Latinx experiences in the US church.

In his book, *PADRES: The National Chicano Priest Movement*, Richard Edward Martínez highlights the differences between these experiences of immigration. "During the late nineteenth and early twentieth century, large waves of Catholics immigrated to the United

States from Ireland, Italy, Germany and Poland. Each group arrived with its own priests and religious leaders who established parishes, schools and hospitals, which serviced the respective ethnic enclaves."[3] For the Mexican community, it was a different experience of church: "[B]etween 1848 and 1960, the church effectively functioned as a partner in the colonization process by helping to maintain the racial and capitalist order in the Southwest. This was accomplished in part by the infliction of daily indignities, the administration of bourgeois theology, cultural oppression, and the elimination of native Mexican American clergy."[4] After the Treaty of Guadalupe Hidalgo was signed in 1848, incorporating much of the Southwest into US territory, the American Catholic Church quickly sought to eliminate Mexican clergy and imposed European bishops and priests. In a letter dated February 1, 1852, the newly assigned French Bishop Jean-Baptiste Lamy wrote shortly after his arrival in New Mexico, "I pray that these Mexican clerics would leave soon, and the sooner the better."[5] It is important to note that the treatment of the Mexican people was anything but Christian. They were pushed to the backs of churches and into basements; because of the color of their skin, they were denied burials in Catholic cemeteries and "access to white Masses. . . . The homily was partially bilingual, fifteen minutes in English and five minutes in Spanish."[6] They were treated as second-class citizens not only in society but even in the church.

In the aftermath of the Second Vatican Council, there arose among Latino and Latina religious leaders a new consciousness about what it meant to be Hispanic in ministry in the US church. PADRES (Padres Asociados para Derechos Religiosos, Educativos, y Sociales/ Priests Associated for Religious, Educational, and Social Rights), a Chicano priests' organization, was formed in 1969. Later, in 1971,

---

3. Richard Edward Martínez, *PADRES: The National Chicano Priest Movement* (Austin, TX: University of Texas Press, 2005), 4.

4. Martínez, *PADRES*, 5.

5. Lamy, Letter, 1 February 1852, Archives of the Archdiocese of Santa Fe, Folio No. I, cited in Luciano C. Hendren, "The Church in New Mexico," in *Fronteras: A History of the Latin American Church in the USA since 1513*, ed. Moises Sandoval (San Antonio, TX: Mexican American Cultural Center, 1983), 198 cited in Martínez, *PADRES*, 10, see n. 33, 156.

6. Martínez, *PADRES*, 6.

Las Hermanas (The Sisters) was established.[7] PADRES fought against the injustices and grave ills suffered by la comunidad latina in the West and Southwest regions of the country. They were influenced by the work of César Chávez and fought with him in many instances for justice. Founded in San Antonio, this national association of Mexican-American clergy sought to translate "the cry of our people to the decision-makers of the Catholic Church in America."[8] Their influence and pressure reached the decision-making body of the hierarchy, and Fr. Patricio Flores was named bishop of San Antonio and ordained on May 5, 1970. These pioneer movements of Latino priests and Latina religious modeled prophetic resistance in ways that insisted on inclusion and voice for those made voiceless and pushed to the margins in church and society.

In New York and the Northeast, there was a group of migrants arriving in the US mainland who were citizens yet perceived this new land as a foreign country and were often treated as aliens. Much like the Mexicans in the Southwest and West, Puerto Ricans endured racism, injustice, and exclusion. They too were regarded as second-class citizens. They brought no clergy of their own, in part because of the historical consequences of Spanish colonization and practices that had excluded the cultivation of indigenous or African diasporic clergy. "Most of the clergy ministering to them on the Island of Puerto Rico were from Europe or North America."[9] With the US colonization of the island after the Spanish-American War, from 1899 until January 1964 even the bishops for the Diocese of Puerto Rico in San Juan were non-Puerto Ricans from the United States.[10]

By the 1950s, a steady stream of economically motivated migration from the island resulted in an influx of Puerto Ricans to the Archdiocese of New York. This pastoral reality led the archbishop

7. For an in-depth study of this movement of Latina religious women see Lara Medina, *Las Hermanas: Chicana/Latina Religious-Political Activism in the U. S. Catholic Church* (Philadelphia, PA: Temple University Press, 2004).

8. Cited in Martínez, *PADRES*, 55 from local newspapers, *San Antonio Light* and *San Antonio Express News* (October, 10, 1969), see n. 28, 161.

9. Joseph P. Fitzpatrick, SJ, *The Stranger Is Our Own: Reflections on the Journey of Puerto Rican Migrants* (Kansas City, MO: Sheed & Ward, 1996), 60.

10. "Past and Present Ordinaries," Archdiocese of San Juan de Puerto Rico, http://www.catholic-hierarchy.org/diocese/dsjpr.html, accessed on November 4, 2017.

of New York, Francis Cardinal Spellman, "to follow a policy of what he called the 'integrated' parish, namely, his priests would learn Spanish and become familiar with the background of Puerto Rican culture, and minister in Spanish to the Puerto Ricans."[11] Toward this end, archdiocesan clergy studied Spanish on the island, and no national Puerto Rican parishes were established.

Among the advocates for the Puerto Rican community in New York was a scholar-priest, Fr. Joseph Fitzpatrick, SJ, a Harvard graduate and sociologist on the faculty of Fordham University. Fitzpatrick viewed this internal migration "through my own youthful sociologist's eyes as yet another coming of immigrant people to the United States."[12] He urged his contemporaries to remember their own immigrant roots: "As children of immigrants ourselves, if we reflect on the experience of our own people, we should be best prepared not to make the mistake of judging the Puerto Ricans in the unjust way in which our people were judged themselves."[13] His scholarship revealed both careful study and a pastoral heart. He learned to accompany a people not his own through their joys and sorrows, with a love and affection that was reciprocated. Writing about the celebration of the Golden Jubilee of his priestly ordination, he recalled, "It was an unforgettable day, one which made me aware of how many people greatly appreciated what I had tried to do, and how much gratitude I owed to all of them."[14] Like the priests of PADRES, he assisted this migrant community when it came to matters of policy and politics, religious and educational advances. His commitment was evident not only in his research but also in his homilies, which challenged parishes, academic communities, and Catholic organizations to recognize, include, and respect their Puerto Rican brothers and sisters.[15] In his own way, he modeled prophetic resistance as a priest and scholar who chose to accompany a marginalized community external to his own social location. His limitations

11. Fitzpatrick, *The Stranger*, 60.

12. Ibid., 3.

13. Ibid., 99.

14. Ibid., 88.

15. For example, see Fitzpatrick, "A Plea for Christian Unity," Sermon, *World Sodality Day*, Fordham University, May 10, 1953, in Fitzpatrick, *The Stranger*, 103–106.

and privilege cannot be dismissed, yet neither can his steadfast commitment to justice for the Puerto Rican community in society and the church.

Prophetic Priesthood, Lessons from the Movies

My development of the concept of prophetic priesthood is nurtured by examples like the clergy of PADRES and the scholar-priest Joseph Fitzpatrick. My imagination in this area is further stimulated by three distinct images of priesthood drawn from cinema.

My family and I began to understand the United States through the lens of such films as *West Side Story*, with the Puerto Rican actress Rita Moreno, and the US church through films like *The Bells of St. Mary's* with Bing Crosby as the genial Fr. Chuck O'Malley and Ingrid Bergman as Sr. Mary Benedict, the mother superior. Throughout the film, O'Malley and Sr. Mary express competing theories of education in relation to specific issues that arise with respect to the school and its students. While they often DO NOT agree on tactics or strategies, what is communicated on the big screen is the kindness and pastoral care of the church's priests and sisters. This resonated with my own experiences in the local parish. As a Latino living with daily reminders of racism and exclusion, my surviving and thriving in the midst of struggle was connected to the commitments of these priests and religious women to the well-being of young people like me. Prophetic priesthood is lived in daily accompaniment, especially in options made for the most vulnerable.

As a child growing up, I remember going to Spanish language movies on Sundays after the noon Spanish Mass. One of my favorites was the popular comic actor Mario Moreno, known professionally by his screen name of Cantínflas. In 1964, he appeared as a priest in a comedy entitled *El padrecito*, directed by Miguel M. Delgado. The plot revolved around Fr. Sebastían, a young priest seeking to conscientize his parishioners on matters of social responsibility and justice. At one point, he is engaged in a conversation at table with the pastor and two women, both of whom appear to be church employees, perhaps a secretary and housekeeper. During the meal, the pastor raises his concerns about what Sebastían is teaching in his

catechism classes with the children. When one of the women questions whether he is teaching communism, he responds by quoting
Rerum Novarum, the 1891 social encyclical of Pope Leo XIII. There
is much to unpack in this scene, let alone the film, but a couple of
points are worth noting: the role of the women as equal participants
at table and conversation; and the use of a papal encyclical on labor
and justice in a Mexican comedic film. The proximity of this film to
Vatican II and its reflection on themes of Catholic social teaching,
especially pertinent in Latin America at the time, seem more than
coincidental. The prophetic dimension of priesthood portrayed in
the film was not lost on a Latin American seminarian who wrote the
actor to let him know of the reaction of five hundred of his classmates to a special showing of the film at the time of the council.
They declared it to be "the finest sermon of the modern era," an
affirmation of a rejuvenated church whose priests seek to live evangelization authentically.[16]

A third influential film is the 1989 movie *Romero*, starring Raúl
Juliá, the Puerto Rican actor, in the title role of archbishop of San
Salvador, and directed by John Duigan. The biopic follows Óscar
Romero into his understanding and uneasy embrace of his prophetic
role. One of the most powerful and chilling scenes occurs near the
end as the archbishop addresses a part of his homily toward the military. "No soldier is obliged to obey an order contrary to the Law of
God. In His Name and in the name of our tormented people who
have suffered so much, and whose laments cry out to heaven: I im-
plore you! I beg you! I ORDER you!! STOP THE REPRESSION!!!"[17]
Juliá's delivery of Romero's words invokes chills in the listener, and
the director employs cinematography and music to underscore the
tension and inevitability of Romero's assassination. Ana María Pineda
reminds us that in his prophetic ministry as archbishop, such preaching was typical. "Romero's homilies continued to address the increasing violence and repression. He consistently presented the events in
the light of the Word of God and the documents of the Church such

16. Jeffrey M. Pilcher, *Cantínflas and the Chaos of Mexican Modernity*
(Wilmington, DE: Scholarly Resources, Inc., 2001), 195.

17. "Romero (1989)," American Rhetoric Movie Speeches website, http://
www.americanrhetoric.com/MovieSpeeches/moviespeechromero4.html. Audio
available.

as those of the Second Vatican Council, Medellín, and Puebla."[18] This man of God would not be deterred and continued his prophetic preaching until the end, when he paid the ultimate price with his life. Prophetic priesthood is not lived without risk.

Prophetic Priesthood

Prophetic priesthood is rooted in prophetic resistance, resistance that arises from within communities that have experienced marginalization and exclusion. Prophetic resistance occurs in the daily accompaniment of communities, sometimes communities that are not our own. Prophetic priesthood as authentic evangelization is not without risk and, when lived in resistance as Romero did, can be among the "finest sermons" of our era. These are the lessons that I learned from the cuentos of my familia, from the stories of mi gente, from the movies. These are the lessons that I learned from the story of my father, who would not succumb to the grave injustices of his time. These are the cuentos that continue to nurture my priesthood.

Along with this type of nurturing, there are the Claretian cuentos of prophetic witness and resistance that have been passed on to me, as a Claretian missionary. These courageous stories have been instrumental in shaping my life. I am privileged to share a history with a community that seeks to embrace the prophetic and missionary identity of Jesus. My own eyes have witnessed, firsthand, the US and global impact of my Claretian brothers. This not only encourages me in the everyday, as I accompany the "other," but it also reminds me that I am not alone and that what I do matters in the building up of the reign of God. So, whether I am in the halls of the United Nations or on the Yale University campus or teaching in a graduate school of theology and ministry, I am a missionary priest and preacher who wholeheartedly desires to imitate Jesus the prophet as I am sent out into the world.

18. Ana María Pineda, *Romero and Grande: Companions on a Journey* (Hobe Sound, FL: Lectio Publishing, 2016), 91.

## Chapter 11

A *Bamboo* Priest: An Asian-American Way of Religious Priesthood

VănThanh Nguyễn, SVD

I felt called to the priesthood at a very early age. Already at twelve years old, I began imitating priests by dressing up like them and mimicking various parts of the Mass in front of my cousins. By the age of fourteen, I became more serious in wanting to be a priest by joining the vocation awareness group to pray and discern for God's call. This led me to sign up for a "Come and See Retreat." Together with twenty other Vietnamese youngsters, I spent a weekend of vocation discernment at Saint Augustine's Seminary (run by the Society of the Divine Word, or SVD) in Bay St. Louis, Mississippi. I instantly felt at home and knew exactly what I wanted to be for the rest of my life. At the end of that summer in 1979, I enrolled and was accepted into Saint Augustine's Seminary. I was only fifteen years old, but I knew then that I had found my life's vocation to become a missionary priest. Admittedly, my understanding of the identity of the religious priesthood was quite unclear. Most candidates at that time who chose to join clerical religious congregations wanted to be *just* priests. Like most of them, I was totally ignorant of the distinctiveness of the religious priesthood. As I look back almost forty years later, I have come to a greater appreciation of the missionary and religious formation that has helped shape and influence my identity as a religious priest. The question of importance is: "What does the identity of an Asian-American religious priesthood consist in?" For starters, it is by not being *just* a priest!

Not *Just* a Priest

Somewhere in my formation years as a Divine Word missionary, I stopped wanting to become *just* a priest. The exposure to different missionary and cross-cultural experiences and the ongoing awareness of the religious and missionary aspects of the SVD charism gradually helped fashion my identity as a religious priest. I would like to briefly highlight three important features of that identity.

The first and most important feature of a religious priest is the radical commitment to the three evangelical counsels of poverty, chastity, and obedience. Judith A. Merkle states, "The life of the vows is a central symbol of religious life. The vows symbolize that religious life is a vocation; that is, the individuals who enter into it do not create the terms and conditions of their commitment entirely by their own will."[1] Choosing to live these vows is a response to Jesus' invitation to follow him more closely and intimately. It is true that the Second Vatican Council emphasizes the call of all people to holiness. By undertaking the vows of poverty, chastity, and obedience, however, the religious priest wishes to reach the fullness of Jesus' invitation to a radical discipleship in all its character and dimensions. Fr. Jose Kuriedath poignantly writes, "Even though canonically or legally, one becomes a religious when he/she fulfills the legal requirements of formation or training, and commits oneself through the vows, essentially or internally one becomes a consecrated religious only when one has grown in discipleship and manifests the personality of Jesus in oneself more clearly and powerfully."[2]

Fr. Kuriedath makes a strong case by pointing out that radical or mature discipleship is the foundation or prerequisite for becoming a genuine religious. For example, Jesus chose the Twelve (Luke 6:13-16) and the Seventy-Two (Luke 10:1) out of a larger number of disciples for a special mission; furthermore, when a disciple has been

1. Judith A. Merkle, *Committed by Choice: Religious Life Today* (Collegeville, MN: Liturgical Press, 1992), 79.

2. Jose Kuriedath, CMI, "Vocation to Religious Priesthood: Challenges and Threats," in *Consecrated Life: A Call to Wake Up the World*, ed. Peter Kannampuzha (Kerala, India: LRC, 2016), 185.

chosen, that one—for example, Peter—is asked to love more intensely and faithfully than "all the rest" (see John 21:15-17). In short, the aim of a vowed life is to give religious priests the opportunity to grow and to become mature and radical disciples.

Religious priesthood is a calling, and those who opt for this lifestyle make a conscious choice to live in community. Living in community is the second most important characteristic of a religious priest. Judith A. Merkle writes,

> The vowed life is communitarian. Community is more than a collection of individuals who live private lives and share only leisure activities and selected interests. Rather, community is a life group where one learns to move out of self toward others in love. Through their vows, religious radically bind their lives not only to God and the people of the Church, but also to the welfare of the concrete others in community. It is a bond which is "another kind of love," sealed not by the genital bonding of marriage but by a bond of affection meant to last a lifetime.[3]

Those of us who live in community are fully aware of the blessings and challenges that community life brings. Each one of us is unique. We often come from different countries and therefore have different customs and ways of doing things. We embody diverse worldviews and have developed different habits. Despite our diversity, we intentionally choose to live together as committed disciples seeking a common purpose: to transform ourselves and the world. Moreover, we often set aside our own aspirations, independence, and individualism for the sake of the community and the congregation's charism. Undoubtedly, the charism of one's congregation is an important dimension of one's religious identity.

This leads to my third point. Each religious community has its own charism or cluster of charisms that help shape a *particular* way that a man lives out the ministry of priesthood in the church. For example, as a Divine Word missionary, I am trained to become an intercultural minister for an intercultural mission. Interculturality is a distinct

3. Merkle, *Committed by Choice*, 24.

characteristic of who I am as an SVD.[4] The SVD congregation is deeply committed to and has a long history of striving towards interculturality among its members and in its work. We have even developed cross-cultural programs aiming to produce broad intercultural competence. For an international congregation consisting of about six thousand male religious serving and working in more than sixty nations, interculturality is a necessary component of life and mission and thus has become an essential component of the SVD identity. Divine Word missionaries are intentionally multicultural in their composition as a witness to the world of the universality of the Gospel message. The commitment to live and share intercultural life and mission is a key element of our identity. Consequently, SVD formation (both initial and ongoing) seeks to create an intercultural missionary community that models itself after the Trinity.[5] Having moved beyond a community simply of multiculturalism, we seek to build an atmosphere in our community that mutually respects the richness of every culture and background. We work at it reflexively. We celebrate our differences easily because of our grounding in a tradition that respects and encourages this gospel value. In his keynote address at the 2017 PanAm General Assembly at Techny, Illinois, Fr. Stephen Bevans, SVD, zeroed in on the theme of "Intercultural Leadership for Intercultural Living and Mission." He stated, "Intercultural mission is the only kind of mission there is, and intercultural living the only kind of real life there is. This is a mission and life that calls for wise and skillful leadership—to inspire us to live interculturally and to inspire others to intercultural living as well."[6]

In short, when a religious priest who is committed to the three evangelical counsels makes a conscious decision to live in community

---

4. For many excellent articles, see the following two volumes edited by Lazar T. Stanislaus, SVD, and Martin Ueffing, SVD: Vol. 1: *Intercultural Living* and Vol. 2: *Intercultural Mission* (Sankt Augustin, Germany: Steyler Missionswissenschaftliches Institut, 2015 and 2016).

5. *SVD Constitutions* 501.

6. For an excerpt of Stephen Bevans's address, see the SVD's newsletter, "Arnoldus Nota," October 2017, 4–5. A short video/PowerPoint presentation of his talk is available at https://vimeo.com/ctufaculty/review/234844198 /5119a156d8 (accessed on October 26, 2017).

and to become an intercultural minister for an intercultural mission, he ceases to be *just another priest* and becomes an authentic religious priest who is radically living out his religious vocation—one that is both countercultural and prophetic. But the question remains, "How is this different or distinct for Asians?"

Harmony through Dialogue and Prophecy

To be Asian is to be in harmony. Harmony is essential to the Asian character and personality. Thomas C. Fox succinctly notes, "The notion of harmony shows up in various ways in Asia, for example, in medicine and the belief in the need to maintain a healthy balance of body, mind, and spirit. Yoga teaches that a healthy body, mind, and spirit are one. In Asian symbols, the Yin and Yang teach endless interdependence and larger ineffable unity."[7] Recognizing it as the hallmark of Asians, the Federation of Asian Bishops' Conferences (FABC) affirms that harmony represents "the intellectual and affective, religious and artistic, personal and social soul of both persons and institutions in Asia."[8] Peter C. Phan further clarifies, saying, "Harmony is not 'an absence of strife.' Nor is it merely a pragmatic strategy for common living amid differences."[9] Rather, Phan says, quoting FABC, it is "an Asian approach to reality, an Asian understanding of reality that is profoundly organic, i.e., a world-view wherein the whole, the unity, is the sum-total of the web of relations, interaction of the various parts with each other, in a word, harmony, a word that resonates with all Asian cultures."[10] Basically, harmony is a central spiritual value that is deeply rooted in the souls of Asians.

7. Thomas C. Fox, *Pentecost in Asia: A New Way of Being Church* (Maryknoll, NY: Orbis Books, 2002), 42–43.

8. *For All the Peoples of Asia*, 2:232. Quoted in Peter C. Phan, *Being Religious Interreligiously: Asian Perspectives on Interfaith Dialogue* (Maryknoll, NY: Orbis Books, 2004), 123.

9. Phan, *Being Religious Interreligiously*, 123.

10. *For All the Peoples of Asia*, 2:276 (no. 3.4). Quoted in Phan, *Being Religious Interreligiously*, 123.

The quest for harmony is emphasized in the teachings of most Asian religions, such as Hinduism, Buddhism, and Confucianism. Phan writes, "In Confucianism, harmony must be first realized in the individual by observing five relationships properly: between ruler and subject, between husband and wife, between parent and child, between elder sibling and younger sibling, and between friend and friend. Each of these five relationships implies a set of duties and obligations that must be fulfilled in the manner proper to one's situation in life."[11] The document *Asian and Pacific Presence: Harmony in Faith*, which was developed by the Committee on Migration of the United States Conference of Catholic Bishops (USCCB), affirms that harmony is central both to the lives and cultures of Asia and to Christianity. It states, "Harmony is authentically Christian and intrinsically Asian. Harmony draws its inspiration and strength from the harmonious relationship of the Trinity. Asians and Pacific Islanders teach a threefold harmony: (1) harmony with a personal God, the source of all genuine harmony; (2) harmony among all people; and (3) harmony with the whole universe."[12]

For universal harmony to be achieved, sincere and humble dialogue among all people and religions must take place. Edmund Chia, a theologian from Malaysia who currently teaches at the Australian Catholic University in Melbourne, notes that throughout the thirty years of FABC's existence the theme of dialogue surfaced at practically every assembly and appeared in every document. Chia writes, "Dialogue is the way of being Church in Asia. Dialogue is also the method for doing theology in Asia. In short, dialogue is the life and mode of the Asian Church."[13] Not surprisingly, the FABC emphasizes three areas of dialogue: *with the Asian poor, with their cultures*, and *with their religions*. This "triple dialogue" is the modality in which the church in Asia carries out its "evangelizing mission and

11. Phan, *Being Religious Interreligiously*, 124.

12. See http://www.usccb.org/issues-and-action/cultural-diversity/asian -pacific-islander/resources/harmony-in-faith-sharing-gifts-and-promoting -harmony.cfm (accessed on October 31, 2017).

13. Edmund Chia, *Towards a Theology of Dialogue* (Bangkok, Thailand, 2003), 230. Chia served as executive secretary of interreligious dialogue for the Asian Bishops' Conference from 1996 to 2004.

thus becomes the local church."[14] At every moment of the triple dialogue, a fourfold element is drawn into the conversation:

a. The *dialogue of life*, where people strive to live in an open and neighborly spirit, sharing their joys and sorrows, their human problems and preoccupations.

b. The *dialogue of action*, in which Christians and others collaborate for the integral development and liberation of people.

c. The *dialogue of theological exchange*, where specialists seek to deepen their understanding of their respective religious heritages, and to appreciate each other's spiritual values.

d. The *dialogue of religious experience*, where persons, rooted in their own religious traditions, share their spiritual riches, for instance, with regard to prayer and contemplation, faith, and ways of searching for God or the Absolute.[15]

Recognizing the importance of harmony through dialogue, the Asian bishops encouraged the presbyters to be formed and well trained to carry out the triple dialogue when working and serving in an Asian context. According to the Asian bishops, the role of the presbyter is

> to inspire, to encourage, to foster initiatives, and to help charisms to develop. After the pattern of Christ the Good Shepherd, whose saving action he makes present to his flock, the presbyter is sensitive to its diverse needs, especially those of the underprivileged and the poor. He is quick to come to their assistance and to be

14. Peter C. Phan, *In Our Tongues: Perspectives from Asia on Mission and Inculturation* (Maryknoll, NY: Orbis Books, 2003), 18. See also Phan's latest book, *The Joy of Religious Pluralism: A Personal Journey* (Maryknoll, NY: Orbis Books, 2017), in which he relates his story of the questions raised by the Congregation for the Doctrine of the Faith about his understanding of the salvific role of Christ and the church. In this "page turner," Phan explains the "errors and ambiguities" that were identified by the Vatican in his book *Being Religious Interreligiously*. I highly recommend that everyone read Phan's latest book, *The Joy of Religious Pluralism*.

15. *For All the Peoples of Asia*, FABC Documents from 1992–1996, vol. 2, ed. Franz-Josef Eilers (Manila: Claretian Publications, 1997), 21–26, quoted in Phan, *In Our Tongues*, 19.

present to them in moments of crisis, not content with showing solicitude but being deeply involved in their life and sharing their lot. His one concern is to form his community into a living sign of the presence in the world of the Risen Lord Who assumes and heals all human situations and brings to fulfillment all hopes and aspirations. The *prophetic* role of the presbyter, then, consists in building up a committed Christian fellowship as a *prophetic* sign of the future kingdom already operative in the world.[16]

 Interestingly, the way of being and ministering in the church in Asian contexts is seeking harmony through *dialogue* and *prophecy*. In other words, dialogue alone is not enough; both dialogue and prophecy are important characteristics of a religious priest working in an Asian context. To put it in another way, Asian priests carry out the mission of the church when they live and minister in "prophetic dialogue," a term used to describe the way SVDs engage in mission.[17] This term, or concept, has been well developed by Stephen Bevans and Roger Schroeder. Their book, titled *Prophetic Dialogue: Reflections on Christian Mission Today*, has further clarified this important characteristic and has greatly contributed to the field of mission theology. Moreover, I believe that Asian religious priests, in the context of the community and charism of their particular congregation, can easily embrace prophetic dialogue as a way of being religious today. Consequently, harmony through dialogue and prophecy is an appropriate modality and characteristic of Asian religious priesthood today.

A Bamboo Priest—A Unique Way of Being Religious

Bamboo trees[18] grow everywhere in Asia. Many villages throughout the countryside of Asia are filled with beautiful and evergreen bam-

---

16. *For All the Peoples of Asia*, FABC Documents from 1970–1991, vol. 1, ed. Gaudencio B. Rosales and C. G. Arevalo (Manila: Claretian Publications, 1997), 86 (emphasis added).

17. Stephen B. Bevans and Roger P. Schroeder, *Prophetic Dialogue: Reflections on Christian Mission Today* (Maryknoll, NY: Orbis Books, 2011), 59.

18. Technically, bamboo belongs to the Bambusoideae subfamily of the perennial evergreen grass family Poaceae. See https://www.britannica.com/plant/bamboo.

boo trees. They often form a protective barrier or wall for houses and villages. Bamboos are some of the fastest growing plants on earth, with some types growing as much as 30 centimeters (1 foot) per day. Particularly in Southeast Asia, bamboos have notable economic and cultural significance. They are used for building materials, as a food source (for example, bamboo shoots), and as a versatile raw product. Bamboos are known for possessing more compressive strength than wood, brick, or concrete and a specific tensile strength that rivals that of steel. The fine-grained silica produced in the joints of bamboo stems has been used as medicine for healing. Other common usages of bamboo include fine-quality paper, furniture, flooring, walking sticks, fishing poles, garden stakes, chopsticks, musical instruments, weapons, writing tools, and knitting needles. Needless to say, bamboos are known for their utility and beauty and are often celebrated in paintings and poems. Consequently, allow me to use this image—the symbolism of bamboo—to underscore the character and qualities of Asian religious priests. There are several lessons that Asian religious priests can learn from bamboo.

1. Strength

Bamboos are not known for their size. Even the largest type of bamboo is nothing compared to the big oak or pine trees in the forest. Nevertheless, bamboo plants can endure cold winters and extremely hot summers that many other bigger trees cannot, and they are often the only trees left standing in the aftermath of a storm. An extraordinary example of bamboo's resilience is the fact that they were the only plants to survive the radiation of the atomic bombings in Hiroshima, Japan, in 1945. The incinerating heat destroyed all trees and other plant life, except for a grove of bamboos. The grove has since been removed, and some of its remains are preserved in a museum in Hiroshima.[19] The first lesson of bamboo is not to underestimate ourselves or others based solely on perceptions of what is weak and what is strong. One does not have to be big and imposing in appearance to be strong. For example, in the winter, the heavy snow bends

19. See https://www.bambooimport.com/en/blog/facts-about-bamboo (accessed on October 10, 2017).

the bamboo back and back until one day the snow becomes too heavy and begins to fall, and the bamboo snaps back up tall again, brushing aside all the snow. The bamboo can endure the heavy burden of the snow and in the end still have power to spring back. Bamboo has a remarkable ability to spring back after experiencing great adversity. Additionally, the wood of bamboo is incredibly strong and can be tougher than a steel rod. Its strength allows bamboo to stand up straight even though it is only a thin reed. Like bamboo, Asian religious priests can stand tall and believe in their own strength and resilience to overcome all the elements of life and the challenges that might come their way. Furthermore, there is profound strength in kindness, compassion, and teamwork. There is a saying in Vietnamese that speaks very powerfully about cooperation and unity: "Một cây làm chẳng nên non, ba cây chụm lại nên hòn núi cao" ("One tree amounts to nothing; three trees together form a high mountain"). For example, as of 2017, there are approximately 950 Catholic priests of Vietnamese origin in the United States. While the majority of the priests are diocesan, over three hundred priests are religious from about twenty-six men's religious orders, congregations, and institutes.[20] Unquestionably, Vietnamese priests in the United States contribute a lot to the US Catholic Church; however, I believe they could do much more and make a bigger impact on the life and structure of the church if they were able to collaborate better with each other.

2. Flexibility

One of the most notable things about bamboo is how it moves and sways with the wind. While its roots are deep and solid, bamboo can move effortlessly and sway harmoniously with the wind, never fighting against the breeze. In time, even the strongest gust of wind will tire itself out and die down, but the bamboo will remain standing tall and still. This gentle swaying movement is a symbol of flexibility—that is, a "bend-but-don't-break" spirit. What gives the bamboo such remarkably flexibility is its root system that grows horizontally through the dirt, intertwining with the roots around it. Since the roots spread out rather than grow straight down, bamboo holds the

---

20. See https://tuannyriver.com/2017/09/17/how-many-vietnamese -catholic-priests-are-there-in-the-u-s/ (accessed on October 1, 2017).

soil together. This keeps bamboo from being uprooted during a storm and prevents soil erosion. This "bend-but-don't-break" approach is a valuable lesson for religious priesthood today. In a time of constant change, religious priests need to be flexible to bend and adapt to the world around them, yet not break. However, to be flexible enough not to break from the pressure, they must be strongly rooted. As religious priests, they must establish a firm foundation in the charism of their congregation. In an increasingly mobile world, religious today need to make a greater effort to establish their roots in their own and local communities and with their people so that their spirit will not break under the pressure of change. If our roots are deep and inter-connected, religious priests can easily draw on the strength of their religious charism and confreres, who will assist them to weather the trials of life and endure the test of time. Like the bamboo, religious priests today must learn to temper strength with flexibility.

3. *Simplicity*

Bamboo produces neither flowers nor fruit. One anonymous writer compared himself to bamboo, saying, "I will not grow flowers, so that I avoid tempting the butterflies and bees to disturb me." It is no surprise that bamboo has often been used to symbolize the life of simplicity. Furthermore, the hollow insides of bamboo symbolize emptiness and humility. One Chinese artist wrote, "Bamboo, who understands humility by emptying his heart (without stuffing it with arrogance), is my teacher."[21] Simplicity means centering in on that which is important and letting go of the rest. It can mean living with few possessions and entanglements, but more broadly it is an attitude or an approach to life that often leads to greater happiness and free-dom. As in the bamboo, there is great beauty in simplicity. To em-phasize the beauty of the bamboo, allow me to tell a story about its usefulness that more than makes up for its simplicity.

> Less than a year after he developed the first practical light bulb (1880), Thomas Edison designed a new version that had all the essential features of a modern light bulb; an incandescent filament

21. See http://livingartsoriginals.com/flower-bamboo.htm (accessed October 15, 2017).

in an evacuated glass bulb with a screw base. The most critical factor was finding the right material for the filament, the part inside the light bulb that glows when an electric current is passed through it. Edison tested more than 1,600 materials, including coconut fiber, fishing line, even hairs from a worker's beard. Finally, Edison ended up using bamboo fiber for the filament. Edison and his team discovered that carbonized bamboo had the capacity to conduct electrical current, and that it could last more than 1200 hours, more than any other material at the time. Researchers have built upon his work and now have discovered that bamboo charcoal is a natural "nano tube" that can conduct electricity as a very thin film [dispersed] on the surface of a glass or silicon substrate.[22]

"Simplicity," said Leonardo da Vinci, "is the ultimate sophistication." Notably, the simplicity of the bamboo can teach a valuable lesson for Asian religious priests today. Simplicity allows them to consume less, helping them to focus on what is essential rather than getting lost in a clutter of things, possessions, titles, positions, and clericalism. In a world filled with many distractions and constant interruptions, simplicity will help the religious maintain clarity of mind and purpose. Furthermore, the hollow insides of the bamboo can help remind us that we must learn to empty ourselves to serve with integrity and dedication just as Christ "emptied himself, / taking the form of a slave, / coming in human likeness; / and found human in appearance, / becoming obedient to death, / even death on a cross" (Phil 2:7-8). Indeed, Asian religious priests can draw a meaningful lesson from the bamboo.

Conclusion

"Father, you are different, not like the other priests!" I occasionally get this comment from my friends. At first, I was taken aback by their comments, not sure what they really meant. I have come to realize that many of my friends do know the difference between a religious and a diocesan priest, although only in a limited or super-

22. See https://www.bambooimport.com/en/blog/facts-about-bamboo (accessed on November 1, 2017).

ficial way. The challenge for us Asian-American religious priests is to live and carry out our priestly ministry with integrity and to maintain our distinct identity as religious so that we do not become replicas of diocesan priests. To achieve that goal, we must first strive to be priests shaped by the prophetic nature of the vows and the charisms of our congregations, striving—especially in my own case— to be intercultural, countercultural, and prophetic. We are members of our religious congregations *first*, and only then priests within those congregations. Secondly, Asian-American religious priests do well to heed the teaching of the Asian bishops to seek harmony through dialogue and prophecy—in other words, "prophetic dialogue"—as the modality of being, evangelization, and mission. Finally, Asian religious priests can draw valuable and meaningful lessons from the bamboo. While it is only a reed, it has extraordinary strength, amazing flexibility, and surprising simplicity. As a result, being a bamboo priest is a very unique and authentic manner of being an Asian religious priest today.

Chapter 12

The Spirituality of Priesthood in Religious Life

Daniel P. Horan, OFM

Introduction

Unlike a more strictly historical approach to the development of the theology of ministerial priesthood in the Roman Catholic tradition—which is itself a difficult task, given the complex development of the theology of priesthood over two millennia—the exploration of the topic "spirituality of priesthood" as such is further complicated by the ambiguities of the discipline of spirituality.[1] This enterprise becomes all the more challenging when we move from discussion about spirituality in terms of secular or diocesan clergy to talking about "the spirituality of priesthood in religious life," given the plurality and range of traditions of consecrated life, which Paul Hennessy described as a "concert of charisms."[2] Can we really talk

---

1. For example, see Sandra A. Schneiders, "The Study of Christian Discipline: Contours and Dynamics of a Discipline"; Bernard McGinn, "The Letter and the Spirit: Spirituality as an Academic Discipline"; and Walter H. Principe, "Broadening the Focus: Context as a Corrective Lens in Reading Historical Works in Spirituality," in *Minding the Spirit: The Study of Christian Spirituality* (Baltimore: John Hopkins University Press, 2005), 5–24; 25–41; and 42–48.

2. Paul K. Hennessy, *A Concert of Charisms: Ordained Ministry in Religious Life* (New York: Paulist Press, 1997), 7–8. For helpful resources about the spirituality of ministerial priesthood in the secular or diocesan context, see Ronald D. Witherup, *God Tested in Fire: A New Pentecost for the Catholic Priesthood*

about a *singular spirituality* of priesthood in religious life without an exhaustive accounting of each and every spiritual and theological tradition of all forms of monastic, mendicant, and apostolic life? Yes and no.

In terms of the negative, indeed, there is no way to successfully include in a single spirituality all facets and nuances of the diverse expressions of religious life and how each of those communities understands the role of the ordained presbyter within that community. Each order and congregation has its own particular charism, history, and tradition; this prohibits our doing justice to the particularity of each spiritual tradition. And yet there must be something we can identify within the theology of ministerial priesthood that will provide us with a positive trajectory (as opposed to simply stating that the unifying factor is merely that religious presbyters are *not* secular clergy) for considering the spirituality of priesthood in religious life across the spectrum.

I believe that one such starting point for us to consider is an emphasis on the *prophetic office* of the ministerial priest. By virtue of baptism, all the faithful share in the *tria munera*, the threefold office or charism of Christ as priest, prophet, and king. Through sacred orders, ministerial priests exercise the *tria munera* in a particular threefold manner through the sanctifying office (priest), teaching office (prophet), and pastoral office (king). Both secular and religious ministerial priests exercise all three of these offices, but for our purposes here it is worth exploring which of the *tria munera* is emphasized in a place we might rightly identify as first among equals. If we

_____

(Collegeville, MN: Liturgical Press, 2012); Sebastian Kizhakkeyil, *The Priest: Theological Reflections on Priesthood and Priestly Spirituality in Light of Church Teachings* (Bangalore: Asian Trading Corporation, 2010); George A. Aschenbrenner, *Quickening the Fire in Our Midst: The Challenge of Diocesan Priestly Spirituality* (Chicago: Loyola Press, 2002); Stephen B. Bevans, "A Spirituality of American Priesthood, Part I: Resources for Leadership in a Missionary Church," *Emmanuel* 108 (2002): 194–208; Stephen B. Bevans, "A Spirituality of American Priesthood, Part 2: Resources for Leadership in a Missionary Church," *Emmanuel* 108 (2002): 260–75; Paul J. Philibert, *Stewards of God's Mysteries: Priestly Spirituality in a Changing Church* (Collegeville, MN: Liturgical Press, 2004); Michael Heher, *The Lost Art of Walking on Water: Reimagining the Priesthood* (New York: Paulist Press, 2004); and Donald B. Cozzens, *The Spirituality of the Diocesan Priest* (Collegeville, MN: Liturgical Press, 1997), among others.

look to *Presbyterorum Ordinis* (1965) and consider the interesting history of its multiple draftings and revisions, we see that the emphasis is ultimately placed on the sanctifying office as the first among the equal *tria munera*.[3] However, as any close reader of the conciliar document on priesthood will note, the primary subject and audience are secular or diocesan clergy. The council declared: "What is said here applies to all priests and especially to those who are engaged in the care of souls. It is to be *applied to religious priests insofar as its provisions suit their circumstances.*"[4] There is clear recognition that there is something distinctive about priesthood in religious life, even if these ministerial priests share in the same sacred order.

This seeming accommodation for religious, without further exploration or explanation, can be seen as a result of the development of the theology of priesthood from the Council of Trent through the Second Vatican Council.[5] Whereas since Trent, ministerial priesthood was understood primarily in the static terms of one's sacerdotal function in ministry with an emphasis on sacred power (*potestas*), Vatican II in *Presbyterorum Ordinis* shifts the focus toward the concurrent multiple identities (e.g., sacramental, leadership, teaching, *in persona Christi* and *in persona ecclesiae*, etc.). While Vatican II places the sanctifying office or function of ministerial priesthood as the first among equal *munera* for secular or diocesan priests, the council nevertheless bracketed how to understand ministerial priesthood within *religious life*. And this is where the prophetic office comes to the fore.

The Centrality of the "Prophetic Office"

Hans Urs von Balthasar is one of the few theologians in the twentieth century to explore deeply the question of the relationship between the ministerial priesthood and the charism or vocation to religious

---

3. This is perhaps most starkly seen in the full title of the final text: *De Presbyterorum Ministerio et Vita*, in which "ministry" is placed first rather than the *vita*, or lived experience, of the ministerial priest as such.

4. *Presbyterorum Ordinis* 1. Emphasis added.

5. For more on this, see Edward P. Hahnenberg's contribution to this volume as well as Kenan Osborne, *Priesthood: A History of Ordained Ministry in the Roman Catholic Church* (Eugene, OR: Wipf and Stock Publishers, 1989).

life.[6] Von Balthasar's approach to the question of religious priesthood is rooted in broader interest in developing a theology of what he called "states of life," or what we might now identify as a universal call to holiness in keeping with the teachings of *Lumen Gentium*. Each baptized member of the church, regardless of his or her status as lay or cleric, religious or secular, lives out of a particular calling. Regarding members of religious orders, von Balthasar emphasized the "eschatological significance of religious life as a particular charism."[7] For von Balthasar, the particular charism of the tradition into which individual members of religious orders enter by virtue of profession of the evangelical counsels is the source of their primary vocation. This is certainly easy to recognize in women and men religious who are not ordained, but a potential problem arises with those who are also ordained to the ministerial priesthood. Is there a conflict? Is there some kind of compromise? Is the vocation to religious life subjugated to the call and exercise of the ministerial priesthood?

The proposed solution is one in which the exercise of the *tria munera* as ministerial priests does not subsume the religious identity, but instead exists in complementarity (and sometimes tension) alongside and concurrent with religious charism. In thinking about the distinctive state of life found among professed religious, von Balthasar notes that the primary vocation for ordained members of religious communities is *not* reduced to sacramental presidency (i.e., the sanctifying office) but should be grounded in the vocation of religious life reflected in the shared profession of evangelical counsels, community life, and the radical call to follow Christ (*sequela Christi*). In other words, von Balthasar does not reject the reality or importance of the sanctifying office in the exercise of presbyteral ministry within religious life, but instead opens a space for considering a different emphasis in both a theology and a spirituality of priesthood in religious life.

---

6. See Hans Urs von Balthasar, *Explorations in Theology, Vol. 2: Spouse of the Word* (San Francisco: Ignatius Press, 1991). Also, see D. Christian Raab, "Compromise or Charism?: The Identity and Mission of Religious Priesthood in Light of Hans Urs von Balthasar's Theology," (unpublished dissertation, Catholic University of America, 2015).

7. David N. Power, "Theologies of Religious Life and Priesthood," in *A Concert of Charisms*, 82.

This need to consider ministerial priesthood in religious life by starting with each community's respective charism is something that has since been incorporated into the USCCB's *Program of Priestly Formation* (in the fifth edition).[8] In essence, the ministerial priesthood to which both secular and religious clergy are ordained is the same, but in lived reality, the *emphasis* is notably different, as seen in both formation of candidates and the exercise of active ministry.[9] Granting, of course, the coequality of the *tria munera*, Thomas Rausch has proposed that whereas the theology and spirituality of secular priesthood begins with the sanctifying office, for religious clergy it ought to begin with the prophetic office.[10] This can be a difficult task at times because of the loss of the general prophetic dimension of the ministerial priesthood over time, culminating with the Council of Trent's nearly exclusive focus on *potestas* and the sacerdotal dimension of the sanctifying office in contradistinction to the reformers' emphasis on the preaching the Word. This led to the reduction of a dynamic understanding of the ministerial priesthood to a static and cultic understanding of priesthood. With Vatican II, there was a restoration of the prophetic and leadership offices alongside the sanctifying office in the renewed attention to the *tria munera*, which provides a new opportunity to reconsider the spiritual life and vocation of ministerial priests in religious life.

Before we look at what exactly spirituality means and, furthermore, what a *spirituality of priesthood in religious life* might mean,

---

8. See United States Conference of Catholic Bishops, *Program of Priestly Formation*, no. 30, 5th ed. (Washington, DC: USCCB Publishing, 2005), 14: "Centuries of tradition bear witness to a difference between formation for religious life and formation of candidates for the [diocesan] priesthood. Formation for religious life must always take into account the charism, history, and mission of the particular institute or society, while recognizing the human, spiritual, intellectual, and pastoral requirements incumbent upon all who are called to the ministerial priesthood." See also John W. O'Malley, "Diocesan and Religious Models of Priestly Formation: Historical Perspectives," in *Priests: Identity and Mission*, ed. Robert Wister (Collegeville, MN: Liturgical Press, 1990), 54–70.

9. See John W. O'Malley, "One Priesthood: Two Traditions," in *A Concert of Charisms*, 9–24.

10. Thomas P. Rausch, "Priesthood in the Context of Apostolic Religious Life," in *The Theology of Priesthood*, eds. Donald J. Goergen and Ann Garrido (Collegeville, MN: Liturgical Press, 2000), 105–118.

it will be useful to explore briefly the characteristics of the prophetic office in religious life. Thomas Rausch offers four helpful characteristics that provide a substantive frame for considering what it means to talk about the prophetic office in this context. The first is *mobility*, which means that nonmonastic religious communities—at least in the wake of the Vatican II renewal—are called to a sense of itinerancy. This aspect of living out the gospel call to ministry is very different from that of secular or diocesan clergy who, by virtue of their vocation, commit themselves to living within the boundaries of the local church. The notion of mobility as tied to the distinctive state of religious life is rooted in the embrace of the evangelical vow of poverty, which continuously invites religious to surrender appropriative attitudes toward ministries, churches, and so forth. The second characteristic is *evangelization*, which follows from a spirit of mobility and pertains to the fundamental manner of "going out into the world" as ministers of the Gospel. This includes ministering to and living among those people and populations that might not ordinarily find themselves in typical "church-type" parochial ministries.[11] Here, by way of illustration, we might look to historical and practical examples such as outreach to populations on leper colonies as seen in the ministry of Franciscan sister Mary Ann Cope and St. Damien de Veuster on Molokai; HIV/AIDS ministries in the United States in the 1980s and 1990s; the work of the Josephites and Divine Word Missionaries in the segregated American South; education by women religious and Jesuits of historically disenfranchised communities; and so on.[12] The third characteristic of the prophetic office in religious life is *social justice*, which is primarily about putting one's faith into actions. This is not to suggest that secular clergy do not engage in social-justice ministries. Rather, the emphasis on social justice as a key element of religious life is found at the intersection

11. For more on "church-type" versus "sect-type" ministries, see John W. O'Malley, "Priesthood, Ministry, and Religious Life: Some Historical and Historiographical Considerations," *Theological Studies* 49 (1988): 223–58.

12. Also, see José Rodríguez Carballo, "Al servicio de las iglesias locales: Espiritualidad del presbítero religioso," in *Ministros ordenados religiosos: Situación–Carisma–Servicio*, eds. Aquilino Bocos Merino et al. (Madrid: Publicaciones Claretianas, 2010), 223–24.

of the teaching and governing offices of the *tria munera* in which ordained and nonordained members of religious communities exercise their evangelical call. Furthermore, the 1971 Synod of Bishops identified working on behalf of justice as a constitutive dimension of preaching the Gospel, which is by definition at the heart of the prophetic office.[13] Finally, the fourth characteristic is *intellectual life*, which is not in any way a critique of the education or intellectual aptitude of secular clergy. Instead, Rausch notes the historical reality that many religious communities—monastic, mendicant, and, later, apostolic—have been very active, as both leaders in and beneficiaries of academic study and popular education. Whereas historically emphasis on the formation of secular clergy has centered on what was necessary for the proper celebration of and presidency at the sacraments, religious communities generally employed longer formation programs and emphasized continuing education. A focus as a community on the intellectual life serves all three offices—teaching, sanctifying, leading—but particularly benefits the apostolic work of the teaching, or prophetic, office.[14]

With a preliminary sense of the importance and centrality of the prophetic office as starting point for developing and reflecting on a spirituality of priesthood in religious life, we now turn to examine what we mean by "spirituality."

What Does 'Spirituality' Mean?

Renowned scholar of spirituality Philip Sheldrake has noted that, "while all Christian spiritual traditions are rooted in the Hebrew and Christian Scriptures and particularly the Gospels, they are also attempts to reinterpret these scriptural values for specific historical and cultural circumstances."[15] In a sense, what Sheldrake observes about the nature of spiritual traditions echoes the history of the

---

13. Second Ordinary General Assembly of the Synod of Bishops, "The Ministerial Priesthood and Justice in the World" (30 September–6 November 1971).

14. See Rausch, "Priesthood in the Context of Apostolic Religious Life," 112–116.

15. Philip Sheldrake, *A Brief History of Spirituality* (Oxford: Blackwell Publishing, 2007), 2.

emergence of new forms of religious life. The respective charism of each community arises in history in response to a new pastoral need, just as spiritual traditions emerge in response to the particular "signs of the times" in a given era. This sensibility is affirmed by Joann Wolski Conn, who writes that, "while the definition of spirituality may be generic, there are no generic spiritualities."[16] Indeed, there can be no generic spiritualities because there are no generic persons or forms of religious life; each individual and community brings its own history, founding principles, and charism. And yet, given that the heart of Christian spirituality is an interest in understanding a *way of life* more than a set of rules, abstract philosophies, or a list of beliefs,[17] we can explore what it means to talk about forming a way of life—a *spirituality*—that informs our prayer, ministry, and community as it concerns ministerial priests in religious life.

Defining what spirituality is in general has been an effort fraught with difficulty, especially as the academic discipline of spirituality has begun to take greater shape over the last several decades. Debates over what constitutes the proper object of study or the appropriate methodological approach or the primary sources of spirituality remain ongoing and at times contentious. For this reason, despite Conn's observation that any attempt at describing spirituality as such might come across as generic, there is as of yet no consensus around a singular definition of spirituality in the Christian tradition.[18] In order to proceed in exploring what we mean by a spirituality of priesthood in religious life, we have to select a working definition. Among the numerous good possibilities, I find Elizabeth Dreyer's succinct definition of Christian spirituality to be useful for our purposes. She writes:

---

16. Joann Wolski Conn, "Toward Spiritual Maturity," in *Freeing Theology: The Essentials of Theology in Feminist Perspective*, ed. Catherine Mowry LaCugna (San Francisco: HarperOne, 1993), 237.

17. For example, see Lawrence S. Cunningham and Keith J. Egan, *Christian Spirituality: Themes from the Tradition* (New York: Paulist Press, 1996), 7: "Christian spirituality is concerned not so much with the doctrines of Christianity as with the ways those teachings shape us as individuals who are part of the Christian community who live in the larger world."

18. For a survey of no less than two dozen definitions of "spirituality" in the Christian tradition, see Cunningham and Egan, *Christian Spirituality*, 22–28.

"Christian spirituality is the daily, communal, lived expression of one's ultimate beliefs, characterized by openness to the self-transcending love of God, self, neighbor and world through Jesus Christ and in the power of the Holy Spirit."[19]

This effort to summarize spirituality captures the dynamism of a "way of life" that intersects the personal, the communal, and the divine, recognizing the inherent interrelatedness of Christian faith lived in practice. Furthermore, Dreyer's definition moves beyond the pitfalls of more antiquated notions of spirituality that reduce the dynamic encounter with the divine to a static exercise of devotional practice or popular piety. This is especially important when we consider the spirituality of priesthood in religious life as a distinctive "spiritual tradition." As Sheldrake notes, "A 'spiritual tradition' generally implies a great deal more than the practice of a single exercise of piety or devotion. Rather it embodies some substantial spiritual wisdom which differentiates it from other traditions."[20] While well intentioned, much that has been written about the spirituality of priesthood before and even after Vatican II (generally developed with secular clergy in mind) has been reductive, focusing on themes like "eucharistic devotion" or "praying the Office." These themes in themselves are not inherently bad, but fail in practice to live up to Dreyer's more robust and dynamic definition of spirituality that reflects a tradition that informs a Christian way of life.

I believe that an emphasis on the prophetic office as articulated by von Balthasar and Rausch is a starting point for developing a spirituality of priesthood that can be widely shared among the diverse collection of charisms found in the church's manifold religious communities. Just as a complementary or parallel spirituality of priesthood for secular clergy might begin with an emphasis on the sanctifying office, the focus on the prophetic office roots this spirituality in the *tria munera* at once shared by all the baptized yet exercised differently according to one's state of life. Furthermore, given that all ministerial priests, secular and religious, share in the *tria munera* of Christ, this approach to spirituality is not an "add-on"

19. Elizabeth Dreyer, "Christian Spirituality," in *The HarperCollins Encyclopedia of Catholicism*, ed. Richard P. McBrien (San Francisco: HarperCollins, 1995), 1216.

20. Sheldrake, *A Brief History of Spirituality*, 11.

or something introduced from without. Rather, it is an internal starting point or grounding principle that also allows for the correlation, incorporation, and integration of the particular spiritual traditions, histories, insights, and devotions of various communities into a broader and dynamic *way of life*.

Living and Praying the Prophetic Imagination

Just as our brief consideration of the meaning of spirituality recognized the limitations of and ongoing discussions around the definition and study of spirituality, so we must too acknowledge that the notion of the "prophetic" is understood and applied in myriad ways. Colloquially, it is oftentimes used in reference either to some sort of foreknowledge or to a kind of radical stance within society. Theologically and scripturally, those who are recognized as prophetic see the world as it really is and yet, because they are so steeped in the tradition of the Christian narrative, also "see" the world as God intends it to be.[21] Walter Brueggemann addresses this well: "The prophet is called to be a child of the tradition, one who has taken it seriously in the shaping of his or her own field of perception and system of language, who is so at home in that memory that the points of contact and incongruity with the situation of the church in culture can be discerned and articulated with proper urgency."[22] Given the multivalent character of the *tria munera*, the prophetic office can concurrently be described as the teaching office, the preaching office and, in the proper sense, the prophetic office; Brueggemann's description of the meaning of the prophetic stands at the intersection of these converging vectors of this dimension of our Christian call.

21. See especially Niels Christian Hvidt, *Christian Prophecy: The Post-Biblical Tradition* (New York: Oxford University Press, 2007); Joseph Blenkinsopp, *A History of Prophecy in Israel*, rev. ed. (Louisville: Westminster John Knox Press, 1996); and Abraham Joshua Heschel, *The Prophets*, 2 vols. (Peabody, MA: Hendrickson, 2009). See also Daniel P. Horan, "Bonaventure's Theology of Prophecy in the *Legenda Major*: Sources and Interpretations," *Antonianum* 89 (2014): 39–70.

22. Walter Brueggemann, *The Prophetic Imagination*, 2nd ed. (Minneapolis: Fortress Press, 2001), 2.

For ministerial priests in religious life, several questions should arise, including: How do we exercise this prophetic office? How might we become prophets in our time? What is needed to ground us *spiritually* for this way of life?

Bradford Hinze builds on Brueggemann's work in highlighting the importance of the prophetic imagination. He notes: "The prophet is beckoned to perceive, listen, and empathize from God's point of view, to participate in God's solidarity with a people and the created world in complex religious, social, and political situations, and from this vantage point to speak out in God's name to and for these people and the damaged world, and against destructive powers, in the interest of fuller life."[23] This description should resonate with priests in religious life, in no small part because of the very nature of the life itself, governed as it is by the profession of the evangelical counsels. The commitment to gospel life structured by poverty, chastity, and obedience ought to be aimed at perceiving, listening, and empathizing (obedience/*obedire*); solidarity with people in complex situations (poverty/*sine proprio*); and a freedom to speak out against injustice given one's state in life and society (chastity). In committing to a life of ongoing conversion structured by these religious vows, priests in religious life seek in a particular way to walk in the footprints of Jesus Christ, who was himself recognized as participating in the prophetic tradition that included Moses, Elijah, Isaiah, Jeremiah, and others.[24]

It is not enough to *know* the importance of the prophetic office and therefore establish a distinctive spirituality on an intellectual foundation alone. Instead, priests in religious life must develop their *imagination*, which is that means by which Christians are able to recognize the revelation of God and consider the possibility of the in-breaking of God's reign. The development of the Christian prophetic imagination and its connection to the life of prayer is itself modeled after Jesus's own experience, for, as Sandra Schneiders

---

23. Bradford E. Hinze, *Prophetic Obedience: Ecclesiology for a Dialogical Church* (Maryknoll: Orbis Books, 2016), 128.

24. See Sandra M. Schneiders, *Prophets in Their Own Country: Women Religious Bearing Witness to the Gospel in a Troubled Church* (Maryknoll: Orbis Books, 2011), 80.

notes, "Jesus's prophetic vocation was rooted in and expressive of his *mystical life*, the intense contemplative prayer life that the gospels present as the root of his *experiential knowledge of God*."[25] She adds that "Religious Life begins, both corporately and individually, in an experience analogous to the inaugural vision of the Old Testament prophets and of Jesus himself."[26] It is a call that comes from God, and our response as members of religious communities to that call is the profession of our vows.

I believe that Hinze's work in understanding more fully the prophetic nature of the church offers ministerial priests in religious life four guideposts for responding to the challenge of shaping our foundational spirituality. Drawing on the work of Brueggemann before him, Hinze explains that "the prophetic challenge is to energize through a work of the imagination that evokes *repentance, courage, resistance*, and *hope*."[27] To develop a spirituality and foster a way of life for ministerial priests in religious life, it is worth exploring each of these four points through the lens of prophetic imagination.

First, as religious presbyters, our starting point ought always to be one of humility, recognizing our own frailty, sinfulness, and humanity. This spirit and disposition of repentance is not an enterprise pursued for its own pessimistic sake. Instead, as it does for Pope Francis, who identified himself plainly as "a sinner" in his first public interview in Fall 2013, the guidepost of repentance should reflect the reality of our finite, human circumstances without the gloss of superiority or superhuman status.[28] Furthermore, shaping our spiritual discipline and prayer life by starting with repentance opens us up to a place of vulnerability and relationship that is characteristic of our best selves as interdependent members of both our respective religious community and the church as a whole. Our experience of God's mercy in our vocation and lived histories informs our own merciful outlook toward and patience with others. Keeping in mind the whole person of the religious presbyter, we do well to recall that the exercising of our sanctifying and leadership offices as ministerial priests should be

25. Ibid., 92.
26. Ibid., 99.
27. Hinze, *Prophetic Obedience*, 128–129. Emphasis added.
28. For the English translation, see "Pope Francis: The Interview," *America*, September 30, 2013, https://www.americamagazine.org/pope-francis-interview.

shaped by our prophetic grounding in a spirit of repentance and peacemaking. To this end, we might reflect on the question: How does our way of celebrating the sacraments (especially the sacraments of healing) and the way we exercise our leadership follow Christ's model of prophetic vocation? Does it inspire others to do likewise or inhibit them?

Second, a spirituality rooted in the prophetic office of the ministerial priesthood should be courageous. Too often, in the face of real or perceived fear and threat, ministerial priests in religious life—like most men and women—prefer not to "rock the boat," not to challenge actions or whole systems of injustice, and not to risk becoming unpopular or disliked for preaching the liberating Good News of Christ in word and deed. Our courage as religious presbyters in exercising the prophetic office is grounded in the life, death, and resurrection of Jesus Christ. Therefore, a spirituality that includes courage as a central element operates according to what St. Paul calls the "wisdom of God" (1 Cor 1:18-31) as opposed to the "wisdom" or "logic of the world," which means that we are meant to put our faith into action in such a way as to appear foolish to the worldly. And this takes courage. This is not merely a personal or individual task, but a communal and corporate responsibility as well. One of the roles of religious communities is to provide the fraternal support and encouragement to members to go to new places and in new ways to minister to the people of God. What about our prayer life reflects our desire to be more courageous in our Christian witness and ministry? What role does the Holy Spirit play in our spiritual outlook and way of life?

Third, a spirituality of priesthood in religious life should inspire in us, and others, a form of what Hinze calls Christian "resistance." This point of resistance follows from the last characteristic, courage. Those who begin their understanding of the ministerial priesthood with the sanctifying office are perhaps less likely or able to resist the structures and systems of injustice in the local community, seeing their ministerial activity as disconnected from social engagement. In contrast, ministerial priests in religious life should recognize their call to live out their respective community's charism in the church and in the world, especially with and on behalf of disenfranchised individuals and marginalized communities. Among those attitudes and behaviors that we are called to resist stands the inertial temptation to maintain the status quo at all costs and to perpetuate a "we've always done it this way" mode of thinking. The very existence of such rich and diverse religious communities bears witness to the prophetic characteristic of resistance: new ways of life emerge only when individuals and communities avoid the pitfalls of ministering, praying, and living only in the ways we always have. Brueggemann reminds us that prophets "speak in images and metaphors that aim to disrupt, destabilize, and invite others to alternative perceptions of reality through the power of imagination."[29] This should encourage us to reflect on whether and how our prayer and way of life connects us with this tradition of destabilizing and disrupting images and metaphors that point to an alternative perception of reality—that is to say, God's vision for the world.

Finally, a spirituality of ministerial priesthood in religious life is not merely a ministry proclaiming doom and gloom, but a way of life that announces by word and deed God's hope for humanity and all creation. As Schneiders notes, "The prophets strive to energize hope against the helpless despair of the people who succumb to this 'royal consciousness' which makes the oppressive status quo, no matter how unjust, appear to be 'the only game in town.' "[30] Christian hope at the heart of the prophetic office is not merely a Pollyannaish or saccharine outlook on life in the midst of imperfect or even unjust circumstances.[31] True evangelical hope is instead grounded in the same soil as the vocation of ministerial priesthood in religious life; that is, the context of the world-shattering reality of the Christ experience to which we are always called to give witness. In what or whom do we place our hope? What understanding of hope informs our preaching and teaching? How does our prayer and way of life reflect the prophetic orientation toward hope?

29. Walter Brueggemann, *Theology of the Old Testament: Testimony, Dispute, Advocacy* (Minneapolis: Fortress Press, 1977), 625. See also Robert R. Wilson, *Prophecy and Society in Ancient Israel* (Minneapolis: Fortress Press, 1980).

30. Sandra Schneiders, *Buying the Field: Catholic Religious Life in Mission to the World* (New York: Paulist Press, 2013), 474.

31. For more on this theme, see Francis, *Evangelii Gaudium* (The Joy of the Gospel), apostolic exhortation (Vatican City: Libreria Editrice Vaticana, 2013), available online at http://www.vatican.va/evangelii-gaudium/en/.

Conclusion

As noted at the beginning of this chapter, describing a singular spirituality that adequately takes into account the myriad charisms of religious life is an impossible task, but that should not prevent us from considering resources within the Christian tradition to help us develop a spirituality of priesthood in religious life that can serve at least as a starting point for further reflection. I believe that drawing on the *tria munera* and highlighting the primacy of the prophetic office within the presbyteral identity of members of religious communities offers us a multivalent foundation for considering the distinctive vocation and developing a spirituality of the ministerial priest in religious life. What results is a call to reevaluate our way of life—that is, our *spirituality*—through the fourfold lens of repentance, courage, resistance, and hope, so that we may renew ourselves in living and praying the prophetic imagination.

Chapter 13

Ordained Religious in North America: Insights from the Canadian Experience

Timothy Scott, CSB

Introduction

The particular theme of clerical religious life is of interest to me, in part because of the nature of the body for which I work, the Canadian Religious Conference. Unlike the structure in the United States, the leaders of religious communities of both women and men in Canada form a single national conference. I see on a daily basis how gender shapes and informs difference and how, potentially, consecrated women and men in leadership can learn from one another. As we move from the borders of gender to a national border, we have an opportunity to see if another kind of mutual learning is possible: What can Canadian clerical religious learn from the US experience, and vice versa? What insights and benefits can the Canadian experience provide for clerical religious communities in the United States?

I would like to begin with a little history, which is of course always a great teacher. The record of religious life in Canada is essentially coterminous with the history of the country itself. At the outset, we need to remind ourselves that the First Nations population was here first, and while this was a new world for us, for them it was simply the world. In 1608, clerical religious accompanied Samuel de Champlain in his early exploration of the New World and his first contacts with the aboriginal population. The tiny European population in Quebec received the Franciscan Recollects in 1615, followed by the

191

Jesuits in 1625. Capuchin friars came to Acadia in 1633, the Sulpicians to Montreal in 1648.

In the case of women religious, Marie de l'Incarnation established an Ursuline convent in Quebec in 1639. Marguerite Bourgeoys, the founder of the Congrégation de Notre Dame, was ministering in Montreal by 1653. Twenty-five years after the arrival of Marie de l'Incarnation, Monseigneur François de Laval arrived as vicar apostolic, and in 1674 he was appointed first bishop of the Diocese of Quebec. Relations were a bit strained between women religious and the first bishop; as we say in French, *"plus ça change . . ."* I should also point out that the territory of Bishop de Laval's original diocese extended from the St. Lawrence River through central North America to present-day Louisiana.

With Catholicism as the state religion, the French crown decreed that only Catholics could emigrate to the New World. Consequently, the structures of French Catholic life were replicated in New France. Already in the seventeenth century, there were in place both parishes and diocesan clergy. Women religious established the first hospitals and schools, educating both aboriginal and European children. The evangelization of the aboriginal population was the work of first the Franciscans and subsequently the Jesuits. At the time of the conquest of New France by Great Britain in 1760, there were seven religious communities of women, and three of men (the Jesuits, the Franciscan Recollects, and the Sulpicians), all endowed by the French Crown.

Following the conquest, as *les Canadiens* were forced to switch their allegiance from France to Great Britain, much of the clergy chose to return to the mother country. The British governor had forbidden male orders from accepting new candidates or replenishing their numbers from Europe, though this was relaxed following the French Revolution. In contrast, since female religious were not perceived as a threat to the new order, they continued to minister to and, significantly, to recruit new members from the local population. Consequently, in British North America, health care and education continued to be largely Catholic, church-run, and government-funded, but now by the Protestant British Crown.

Largely due to fears that the American revolutionary spirit might spread northward, Catholics in Quebec in the late eighteenth century acquired rights enjoyed nowhere else in the British Empire. In these new circumstances, the Catholic Church and Catholic religious orders became the voice of the French-speaking population, assuming both political and religious authority.

In contrast, British penal laws had prevented the growth of the Catholic population or church institutions in the Thirteen Colonies. I would argue that this very different early history has shaped the different understandings between the two countries of the role of religious communities in the life of civil society to this day.

Through the nineteenth century, the Catholic population in both the United States and Canada grew rapidly. Among others, Irish Catholics settled in significant numbers on both sides of the border. There was also movement between the two countries. I will refer later to the escape of African American slaves into Canada. But I should at least reference an earlier population transfer—that of the Acadians, who in the 1750s were forcibly expelled by the British to be settled in significant numbers in Louisiana. It was an early and shameful example of ethnic cleansing in the British Empire.

In the latter half of the nineteenth century, industrialization provoked a significant movement of French Canadians into New England. This affected the growth of clerical religious communities such as the La Salette Missionaries and the Society of St. Edmund. They were both founded in France but recruited members from the large French-Canadian Catholic community that had emigrated south in search of work.

Having been granted a form of responsible government in 1848, Canada became a dominion of the British Empire in 1867. The result was a country composed of two nations—one French-speaking and Catholic, the other English-speaking and predominantly Protestant— coexisting in a political dynamic that, for its time, was remarkably peaceful. Quebec-based religious orders played a critical role in preserving the French language and Catholic culture, while a very high birth rate in the general population (*"la revanche du berceau,"* or "the revenge of the cradle") largely compensated for the dearth of French-speaking immigrants.

Canada became a refuge for some thirty thousand African Americans up to the end of the Civil War. Those who escaped joined a wave of United Empire Loyalists who had earlier fled north, creating communities whose place names recall their heritage: Negro Brook Road in New Brunswick; Africville in Nova Scotia; Negro Lake in Ontario. Some of these settlers were African American veterans of the War of 1812 who had received land grants in recognition of their service. In Ontario, former African American slaves founded several communities and were at the forefront of the abolitionist cause, producing pamphlets and newspapers that were smuggled south. Later in the century, Charles Uncles became the first African American to be ordained to the priesthood on US soil. He had begun his seminary studies in 1883 in Saint-Hyacinthe, Quebec, because at the time no US seminary would admit him.

In one respect, the United States was ahead of Canada: in 1875, John McCloskey of New York became the first cardinal in the New World. Only eleven years later did Elzéar-Alexandre Taschereau receive the red hat in Quebec. (As an aside, until the 2016 consistory, the only North American cardinal named by Pope Francis had been Gérald Cyprien Lacroix, the archbishop of Quebec and twenty-fourth successor to Msgr. de Laval. While Cardinal Lacroix was born in Quebec, his family moved to New Hampshire when he was a child; he is a graduate of St. Anselm's College in Manchester.)

If we jump ahead to 1960 and the period preceding the Second Vatican Council, it is clear that to a large extent clerical religious life in Canada reflected the country's political culture. Most religious communities (Jesuits, Oblates, Redemptorists, Franciscans) had separate provinces according to the language spoken. There was (and is) a sizeable English-language population in Quebec and an equally large French-speaking population outside of Quebec, but by and large those called to religious life entered into the province of their institute that spoke their mother tongue. To use the famous phrase of Canadian novelist Hugh MacLennan, the "two solitudes" that formed the country, English and French, were very much at work in the organization of clerical religious life.

In Canada, we tend to distinguish our two national groups by the language spoken rather than by culture. French-speaking Canadians are called "francophones"; English-speaking, "anglophones"; and those speaking a different mother tongue, "allophones."

Most people accept a kind of sweeping generalization concerning Quebec history from 1960 to 2000: In essence, the "Quiet Revolution" of the 1960s ended a political culture that was Catholic, clericalist, and backward-looking. There is a term for that past age: *la Grande Noirceur*, "the Great Darkness." It was replaced by a secular nationalism that grew into a movement for political independence and was twice tested in referenda: first in 1980, then in 1995. In the latter case, of 4.8 million votes cast, the "no," or federalist, side won by 54,000 votes, or slightly over 1 percent. The drive for political independence in Quebec put the Canadian episcopate and the leadership of Canadian religious communities in a delicate position. Though both were officially neutral, there were certainly religious and clergy on both sides of the political equation.

Today

In Canada today, there are slightly over thirteen thousand women and men religious; 70 percent are in Quebec, 30 percent outside of Quebec (or, as the statisticians say, in the "ROC"—the rest of Canada); 72 percent are women; 28 percent are men. As executive director, I'm in a double minority—anglophone and male in a conference that is majority female and francophone.

As we compare political cultures on the two sides of the border, it is clear that Canada has secularized at a more rapid rate than the United States and has seen a steeper decline in religious practice. While we tend to use terms like "separation of church and state" in Canada, they are inaccurate, since denominational education is still constitutionally protected and funded in several provinces. Still, the desire for an increasingly secular political culture is more pronounced in Quebec than elsewhere in Canada.

It would be foolish to think that the political concerns expressed today here in the United States do not at least find an echo among your neighbors north of the border. To quote former prime minister Pierre Trudeau, the father of our current leader, in a 1969 address to the National Press Club in Washington, DC: "Living next to you is in some ways like sleeping with an elephant. No matter how friendly and even-tempered is the beast, if I can call it that, one is affected by every twitch and grunt."[1]

What does Canadian secularization look like? It corresponded to the post–Vatican II exodus of priests and religious from active ministry and the collapse of the very large classes of novices and seminarians

---

1. Quoted in Terrance Wills, "Trudeau Fields Hawkish Question and Calls for U.S. Dialogue with Cuba," *The Globe and Mail*, March 26, 1969, 1.

that characterized the postwar decades. Capital punishment was abolished officially in 1976, but the last execution in Canada had occurred much earlier, in 1962. Canada legalized abortion in 1969, four years before *Roe v. Wade*; homosexual acts were legalized that same year. To once again quote Pierre Trudeau: "The state has no business in the bedrooms of the nation."[2]

More recently, in 2005 same-sex marriage was approved in Canada, and a law permitting assisted suicide, or medical assistance in dying (MAID), passed in 2016.

What We Have in Common

I think it is important to point out at the outset that Canadian and American clerical religious have much in common. The challenges of current circumstances described by Pope Francis in his letter for the Year of Consecrated Life are familiar to religious in both countries. "We all know the difficulties which the various forms of consecrated life are currently experiencing: decreasing vocations and aging members, particularly in the Western world; economic problems stemming from the global financial crisis; issues of internationalization and globalization; the threats posed by relativism and a sense of isolation and social irrelevance."[3]

In the face of the very real fear that religious life may disappear in many places, Pope Francis's words at the 2017 Mass for the World Day for Consecrated Life are particularly challenging: "The temptation for survival turns what the Lord presents as an opportunity for mission into something dangerous, threatening, potentially disastrous."[4]

2. Quoted in Geoffrey Stevens, "Bill Overhauls Criminal Code," *The Globe and Mail*, December 22, 1967, 1.

3. Francis, Apostolic Letter to All Consecrated People on the Occasion of the Year of Consecrated Life, November 21, 2014, 3, https://w2.vatican.va /content/francesco/en/apost_letters/documents/papa-francesco_lettera -ap_20141121_lettera-consacrati.html.

4. Francis, Homily on the Feast of the Presentation of the Lord and the 21st World Day for Consecrated Life, February 2, 2017, https://press.vatican.va /content/salastampa/en/bollettino/pubblico/2017/02/02/170202c.html.

The Uncomfortable Reality of Diminishment

In both countries, there has also been a significant effort to fuse or join provinces, including across national borders; just a few examples would include the Jesuits, the Redemptorists, and the Missionary Oblates of Mary Immaculate. The Canadian experience, however, is more complex because of our linguistic duality. In both countries, the vocational decline amongst clerical religious has been partially offset by a sharing of personnel among provinces in parts of the world where there is a larger number of candidates. This has presented challenges both within religious communities and for the people of God who are served. By design or by accident, I think all communities are facing the reality of an intercultural conversation.

I would also suggest that in Canada, government support for denominational health care and education has rendered bishops and priests more accommodating to the broader political culture. There is no Canadian equivalent to the US bishops' document "Forming Consciences for Faithful Citizenship," issued in conjunction with the recent presidential campaign. We have little experience of a bishop publicly opposing Catholic public officials, and none of an official being refused Communion for advocating a position contrary to church teaching. Even on the complex issues of same-sex marriage and euthanasia, the response of the Canadian bishops has been clear and orthodox but not strident. There are certainly different points of view in the Canadian hierarchy, but there is a reticence about being too confrontational with the government of the day. Since 1968 and the advent of Pierre Trudeau, the only elected prime minister of Canada who was not Catholic was the Conservative Stephen Harper, by all accounts a sincere evangelical Christian who governed from 2006 to 2015. But the press considers a politician's religious practice—or family life for that matter—off limits. There is no Canadian First Family.

Elements That Shape the Culture of Clerical Religious Life

So what has gone into shaping this specifically Canadian identity for clerical religious? In parts of English Canada, Catholic schools still enjoy government funding at the primary and secondary level. In the case of tertiary education, the federated college model is distinctly Canadian. Students take most or even all of these courses in a Catholic college, but they receive a degree from the associated provincial university. Public funding for such colleges made the implementation of *Ex Corde Ecclesiae* particularly problematic in the Canadian context.

A second major area is the post–Vatican II missionary experience in the global South. The presence of significant numbers of both francophone and anglophone clerical religious in Haiti and in other countries of the Caribbean, Latin America, Africa, and Asia has shaped the consciousness of our religious communities. I think Canadian religious communities share this with their US counterparts.

Another formative experience has been the presence of clerical and lay religious with aboriginal and Inuit communities in the Canadian North. The Missionary Oblates of Mary Immaculate are responsible for an extraordinary history in western and northern Canada involving the Métis, Cree, Blackfoot, Dene, and Inuit peoples. In large part due to the efforts of Oblate missionaries, the immigration of European settlers into western Canada was mostly peaceful.

A huge challenge on both sides of the border has been the clerical sex abuse crisis. While the John Jay study dealt only with incidents in the United States, there is no reason in the absence of hard data to suppose that Canadian statistics would differ significantly. What does differ, however, is *when* clerical misconduct became a matter of intense public scrutiny. In the United States, the 2002 exposé by the *Boston Globe* transformed a closeted tragedy into a full-blown public crisis, toppling a cardinal and setting the Catholic Church reeling. The comparable situation in Canada was generated a dozen years earlier by the revelation of a long history of abuse at the Mount Cashel Orphanage run by Irish Christian Brothers in Newfoundland. A further key difference was in the way the information was made public: in Canada, a government-sponsored public inquiry gathered evidence from 1989 to 1991 and released its report separately from a church-ordered and well-respected public inquiry. Nine Christian Brothers went to prison following criminal trials. It was the systemic nature of the abuse, and the refusal of church or civil authorities to act despite repeated warnings going back decades, that proved to be brutal for the church's reputation.

The subject of sexual abuse takes us to a more recent issue confronting the Canadian church that is particularly relevant to clerical religious orders: the tragic history of Indian residential schools. From the 1870s to 1996, 150,000 First Nations children were sent to these schools with the express purpose of cultural assimilation. The schools were funded by the federal government but run and staffed by the churches: 60 percent Catholic; 30 percent Anglican; 10 percent others. On the Catholic side, about two-thirds of the administration and staffing was the responsibility of religious communities. Children were forcibly removed from their parents' custody and in many cases subsequently lost contact with their families. There were high levels of disease, malnutrition, and physical and sexual abuse. We estimate that about six thousand children died, sometimes then buried in unmarked graves.

In 1879, Sir John A. Macdonald, Canada's first prime minister, wrote the following:

"When the school is on the reserve, the child lives with its parents, who are savages, and though he may learn to read and write, his habits and training and mode of thought are Indian. He is simply a savage who can read and write. It has been strongly impressed upon myself, as head of the Department, that Indian children should be withdrawn as much as possible from the parental influence, and the only way to do that would be to put them in central training industrial schools where they will acquire the habits and modes of thought of white men."[5]

The underlying assumptions did not change through the century that the schools were in operation: the practice of uprooting and forcibly assimilating First Nations children has been characterized by serious scholars as cultural genocide. In 2008, the federal government apologized formally to First Nations communities for the residential school system and set up a Truth and Reconciliation Commission somewhat modeled on the South African experience.

The hearings that followed were gut-wrenching. Survivors of the residential schools detailed all manner of abuse suffered at the hands

---

5. Truth and Reconciliation Commission of Canada, *Canada's Residential Schools: The History, Part I: Origins to 1939*, vol. 1 (Montreal: McGill-Queens University Press, 2016), 164.

of priests, sisters, and religious brothers. Fifty-four Catholic entities (i.e., religious institutes and dioceses) that were involved in the running of these schools reached an out-of-court settlement with a value of about Can$60 million. In 2015, the Truth and Reconciliation Commission released its ninety-four recommendations, named "Calls to Action," including a demand that Pope Francis make an apology for residential schools on Canadian soil. The issue is under serious consideration in Rome.

Going Forward

So, amid rampant secularity and the challenges of scandal, how are clerical religious doing in Canada today? The linguistic duality still holds in many respects; I certainly live it every day. However, I would be in the minority of priests in Montreal who regularly minister in both languages. Most priests work in one language or the other; there are few bilingual parishes where services are offered in both English and French. English-language speakers are a minority in Quebec, and they are concentrated on the Island of Montreal. In the country as a whole, French-language speakers are in the minority, but terms like majority and minority are not particularly meaningful, either in the church or in civil society. Church and state both live the realities of linguistic duality with built-in protections for the other language in that particular part of the country. I would argue that the two solitudes remain today, but there is a greater understanding across the linguistic divide.

Religious practice and, consequently, vocations to priesthood and religious life, are higher in anglophone than in francophone Canada. There is a discernible uptick in seminary enrollment in English Canada that has yet to repeat itself in Quebec.

Canada is very careful to maintain a linguistic and cultural balance in its choice of bishops and major superiors; an anglophone president of the conference of bishops is always followed by a francophone. Committees of the bishops' conference are always inclusive of members from both language groups. Religious institutes who have members from both language groups will be careful to elect leadership teams reflective of this reality. In the CRC, where I work, despite the significantly larger number of francophone members, we still maintain the linguistic duality in terms of services offered, but in practice this means activities in one or the other of the two languages rather than bilingual activities. Liturgically as well, we tend not to move back and forth between languages; if, for example, there is a conference over several days, we are more inclined to have one celebration predominantly in French and another in English.

Though francophone Canadians with a tertiary education will often have learned English as a matter of course, such is not always the case. It is a source of pride that they can function completely and at all times in French. I do not think that there is a comparable situation here in the United States, but I wonder whether the Spanish-speaking minority may well evolve in such a direction in a generation or two. One is faced with the classic distinction between the melting pot or mosaic characterization of society.

For the most part, both anglophone and francophone Canadians perceive the linguistic duality as a value. Bilingualism is obligatory for advancement in the civil service, in the military, in the national police force, or in business in several areas of the country. While only about 10 percent of anglophone Canadians outside of Quebec speak French fluently, the remaining 90 percent are inclined to have their children enrolled in French immersion schools at least at the primary level. Likewise, many francophone Quebeckers often go to considerable expense to assure that their children are fluent in both languages.

With an estimated 30 million of the 70 million Catholics in the United States being Spanish-speaking, I wonder if the Canadian linguistic duality can inform a conversion that is really only beginning in the United States. Can we foresee in America, a generation from now, circumstances wherein English-speaking parents will be sending their children to Spanish-language immersion schools because they perceive bilingualism as a cultural and economic value?

Because of Canadian health care and government support for institutions run by religious orders in Canada, most institutes are relatively more secure financially than some of their American counterparts. With universal health care and a guaranteed income for senior citizens, there is no need for a national collection to support retired religious.

Spiritually, how do we embrace the future with hope, in the words of Pope Francis? One could take Archbishop Chaput's words about a lighter church and apply them to religious life: we will have "lighter" religious communities—fewer members, greater cultural diversity, a lighter institutional footprint, less social prominence for members, even a measure of opprobrium as a result of the sexual abuse crisis and our collective mishandling of its perpetrators. Pope Francis's remarks in Milan on the need for religious to be leaven rather than a majority are certainly thought-provoking.[6]

A renewed relationship with aboriginal peoples in Canada is definitely occurring. Unfortunately, the numbers of women and men religious ministering today in First Nations communities are relatively modest. However, expressions of aboriginal spirituality, both Christian and non-Christian, are more common. Aboriginal leaders are finding their place in the church through lay ministries and the permanent diaconate.

Another phenomenon in Canada is the presence of "new" communities such as the Companions of the Cross in Ottawa, from whose membership we now have two anglophone bishops. We have not seen in Canada the growth of religious communities of women similar in style to those currently belonging to the Council of Major Superiors of Women Religious in the United States. But Canadian women and men candidates have traveled south to enter communities that are more traditional in outlook. As well, we have seen the growth of mixed communities whose membership includes consecrated persons of both sexes: Madonna House in Ontario and, in Quebec, Famille Marie-Jeunesse and Famille Myriam Beth'léhem. Although canonically they are associations of the lay faithful, it will be interesting to see how these new communities develop on both sides of the border.

As previously indicated, Canada's leadership conference of major superiors has since the 1960s included both women and men. The French Conférences des Religieuses et Religieux en France has moved to this model, as has the Confederation of Latin American Religious. The United States is more the exception worldwide, with separate conferences of major superiors. As I observe the Conference of Major Superiors of Men, the Leadership Conference of Women Religious,

6. See, for example, "Pastoral Visit of the Holy Father Francis to the Archdiocese of Milan" (March 25, 2017), https://press.vatican.va/content/salastampa/en/bollettino/pubblico/2017/03/25/170325c.html.

and the Council of Major Superiors of Women Religious, I perceive a movement towards greater coordination.

Furthermore, I think Canadian clerical religious can learn from their American neighbors about the importance of support from the broader Catholic community. In Canada, we may have become too used to government funding, making the relationship with the broader Catholic community less urgent and Canadian Catholics (frankly) less generous.

Because Canada's only land border is with the United States, we have often spoken with pride about "the world's longest undefended border," and until recently, we have not been particularly alarmed about unauthorized border crossings. Canada has been welcoming of Syrian refugees during the past twenty-four months, and churches and religious communities have been at the forefront in welcoming families, more often than not of the Muslim faith. It remains to be seen if such openness will continue to characterize the Canadian political culture. In the United States, Catholics can be proud of the prophetic stance taken by US religious and clergy in support of undocumented persons.

Conclusion

I would like to conclude by citing not Pope Francis but his predecessor, Pope Benedict XVI, who said this in his homily for the 17th World Day for Consecrated Life on February 2, 2013: "Do not join the ranks of the prophets of doom who proclaim the end or meaninglessness of the consecrated life in the Church in our day; rather, clothe yourselves in Jesus Christ and put on the armor of light."[7]

It was among his final homilies as pope, since he would announce his retirement only nine days later. There are certainly other dimensions we could explore together: monastic and contemplative ordained religious in both countries have a distinct and valued role in the life of our churches. We could also reflect on religious in the episcopate, whom St. Thomas described without irony as passing to

---

7. See http://w2.vatican.va/content/benedict-xvi/en/homilies/2013/documents/hf_ben-xvi_hom_20130202_vita-consacrata.html.

a higher state of perfection (ST II-II, q. 184, a. 7). Taking our distance from the prophets of doom, I am confident that the ministry of ordained religious will continue in both countries and, in God's plan, may flourish.

Contributors

Stephen Bevans, SVD, PhD, is a member of the Society of the Divine Word and professor emeritus of Mission and Culture at Catholic Theological Union, Chicago.

Maria Cimperman, RSCJ, PhD, is a member of the Religious of the Sacred Heart of Jesus, associate professor of Catholic Theological Ethics, and the director of the Center for the Study of Consecrated Life at Catholic Theological Union, Chicago. *= Preface*

Eddie De León, CMF, DMin, is a Claretian Missionary and assistant professor of Pastoral Theology and Preaching at Catholic Theological Union, Chicago.

Anthony J. Gittins, CSSp, PhD, is a member of the Congregation of the Holy Spirit and professor emeritus of Theology and Culture at Catholic Theological Union, Chicago.

Edward P. Hahnenberg, PhD, holds the Jack and Mary Jane Breen Chair in Catholic Systematic Theology at John Carroll University, Cleveland.

Leslie J. Hoppe, OFM, PhD, is a Franciscan friar of the Assumption Province and the Carroll Stuhlmueller, CP, Distinguished Professor of Old Testament Studies at Catholic Theological Union, Chicago.

Daniel P. Horan, OFM, PhD, is a Franciscan friar of the Holy Name Province and assistant professor of Systematic Theology and Spirituality at Catholic Theological Union, Chicago.

vănThanh Nguyễn, SVD, is a member of the Society of the Divine Word, professor of New Testament Studies and holder of the Bishop Francis X. Ford, MM, Chair of Catholic Missiology at Catholic Theological Union, Chicago.

Maurice J. Nutt, CSsR, DMin, is a member of the Congregation of the Most Holy Redeemer, the vice-postulator of the Cause for Canonization of Sr. Thea Bowman, FSPA, and the convener of the Black Catholic Theological Symposium.

John Pavlik, OFM Cap, MDiv, MA, is a member of the Capuchin-Franciscan Province of Saint Augustine and executive director of the Conference of Major Superiors of Men in the USA.

Robin Ryan, CP, PhD, is a member of the Congregation of the Passion and associate professor of Systematic Theology at Catholic Theological Union, Chicago.

Timothy Scott, CSB, SSL, STD, is a member of the Congregation of Saint Basil and is the executive director of the Canadian Religious Conference.

Katarina Schuth, OSF, PhD, is a sister of Saint Francis of Rochester, Minnesota, and professor emerita at the Saint Paul Seminary School of Divinity, University of Saint Thomas, St. Paul, Minnesota.

David Szatkowski, SCJ, JCD, is a member of the Congregation of the Sacred Heart of Jesus who serves as formation director for his community.

Cardinal Joseph Tobin, CSsR, DD, is the archbishop of Newark and the former general superior of the Congregation of the Most Holy Redeemer.

Index